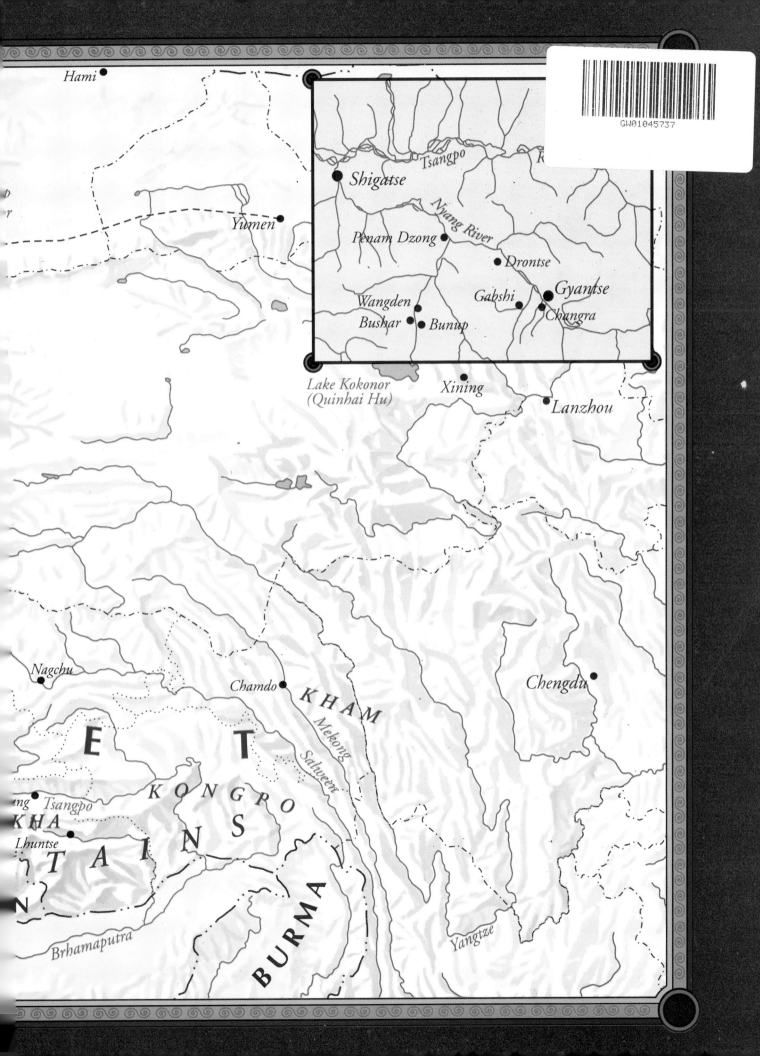

OF WOOL AND LOOM

White Orchid Books

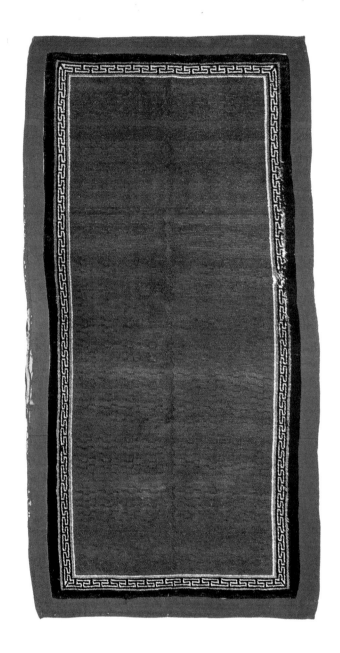

**DEDICATED TO
THE WEAVERS OF TIBET
AND
DOMA G. CHODUN
FOR CONTRIBUTING SO MUCH
TO REVITALIZE THE CRAFT**

OF WOOL AND LOOM

The Tradition of Tibetan Rugs

Trinley Chodrak
and
Kesang Tashi

Orchid Press
Bangkok 2000

Trinley Chodrak and Kesang Tashi
OF WOOL AND LOOM: The Tradition of Tibetan Rugs
First published: 2000
Edited by: Kesang G. Tseten
Photography: Lincoln Potter
Design: Liz Trovato, based on a concept by Luigi Bogni

ORCHID PRESS
P.O. Box 19
Yuttitham Post Office
Bangkok 10907, Thailand

Orchid Press publications are distributed in India and Nepal by
The Variety Book Depot
A.V.G. Bhavan, M3 Con. Circus
New Delhi 11001

This book is printed on acid-free long life paper
which meets the specifications of ISO 9706/1994

ISBN: 974-8304-15-9 (TP)
ISBN: 974-8304-13-2 (HC)

Contents

Sheep grazing at 16,000 feet.

Meditation chamber of
the Dalai Lama at the
Norbulingka, Lhasa.

This book represents a milestone in the dissemination of knowledge of Tibetan art and culture to the West. Although a volume on Tibetan rugs written by Tibetans was published in Lhasa in 1984 (*Bod-kyi grum-ze,* or *Tibet's Carpets*), this is the first book written in the English language by Tibetans about their marvelous and ancient rug tradition.

The literature on this interesting subject is recent and modest. The first book exclusively devoted to Tibetan rugs was Philip Denwood's *The Tibetan Carpet,* published in 1974, the result of a project we started in the early seventies in New Delhi. It was followed by my *Tibetan Rugs* eight years later. In 1984 Diana Myers published an extensively researched exhibition catalogue for the Textile Museum in Washington D.C., titled *Temple, Horseback, Household: Rugs of the Tibetan Plateau.* Since that time, fewer than half a dozen books on Tibetan rugs have seen the light of day, and few of these were published for "the altruistic purpose of sharing knowledge," to use Thomas Cole's apt expression.

In all spheres of scholarship and connoisseurship, the views and insights of informed, native insiders are indispensable, but most often they remain anonymous contributors relegated to footnotes and other scholarly apparatus in ponderous volumes written by outsiders. Here, on the other hand, two distinguished Tibetans not only share their knowledge about a little known aspect of their own culture, but they offer us as well an unusually fine collection of the unknown Tibetan weavers' art. Almost every plate in this book surprises; each invites the reader to undertake a journey into the realms of unexpected symbols, splendid compositions, frivolous as well as subtle color combinations, and even humor.

It has been my fortune, since my arrival in Nepal in 1972 for what was to be a happy seven-year stay with an international organization, to be acquainted with Kesang Tashi's large family. They had established themselves there after leaving Tibet and the family trading business behind. It was a large, generous, and very cheerful family that readily adapted to the small cosmopolitan environment in Kathmandu in those days. Years later, in the early 1980s, contact was re-established with Tashi, then a prosperous but bored banker in New York. We discussed and argued about rugs, wool, sheep, yak, and Tibet. In 1986, I had just returned from my first visit to Tibet, where I had a chance to see close up the people and country and rugs I had read about and written about. I was struck by the optimism of the people and arduous reconstruction work going on in the villages on one hand, and the wealth of highest quality wool being exported raw in bulk on the other hand. Why, I wondered, in an unsolicited report sent to the government foreign economic relations staff in Beijing with whom I had traveled in Tibet, could not these be combined to add value and provide much needed income for the village populations by building on their traditional knowledge and wool-craft skills? The response was not negative, but as I had left Asia in the meantime to return to Norway, it was not possible to accept the suggestion to return.

But Tashi had not been idle, and was considering starting a carpet business in Tibet. We had long discussions on wool grading, wool treatment, vegetable dyeing, traditional designs, flat weaves using yak hair and designing projects that would benefit the people directly and so on and so forth. Tashi had his ideas, and I mine; he was, of course, the more realistic. Eventually, I hammered out a long discourse on the virtues of the traditional colors, design and vegetable dyes, as well as the need to respect Tradition with capital T. I also felt that a village-based system along the lines of the Dobag project in Turkey should be tried out. Tashi, on the other hand, knew the possibilities and limitations of operating in Tibet and China better than me, and set out to establish the Gangchen carpet venture, respecting very much the traditional Tibetan crafts as only a Tibetan can, ignoring the so-called market demands. The rest is history. But Tashi is more than an entrepreneur. He is also a sensitive and perceptive person, with a deep and genuine love for his people and their cultural traditions; his collection of old rugs has been assembled with the objective of preserving and sharing this tradition with others.

Sheep at Nangkhading, near a village called "roof of the sky."

Trinley Chodrak, Tashi's co-author, I do not know personally, but after reading the manuscript and working with Tashi on the book, I feel like I know him very well. He is a man of scholarship and wide experience, and has added immensely to our knowledge through his attention to detail. Much useful and new information added as the manuscript went through draft stages has come from his hand, and Tibetan rug lovers will be grateful for Trinley Chodrak's contribution to Tibetan rug scholarship.

HALLVARD KÅRE KULOY

The annual rug wash on the Tsangpo River.

Rugs woven in Shigatse
for the Gangchen Folk
Arts collection .

I would like to introduce this book by explaining the circumstances that led me to write it. Growing up as a young boy in Tibet, I remember the visual dominance of vividly colorful rugs ornamenting every room in our home. Rugs were also a treasured presence in sacred shrines, assembly halls and in monasteries, particularly in the private quarters of the revered Lamas. I recall that the best rugs were always reserved for the Lamas and the family elders, whether used for decorating their rooms or saddling their horses. Later, when I inherited a few rugs of my own, my interest in these rugs blossomed into more acquisitions. Thus begun my Tibetan rug collection.

For me, collecting Tibetan rugs has been tremendously pleasurable and gratifying. First of all, Tibetan rugs, as you will see in the illustrations throughout this book, are incredibly varied in design, color, appeal, and function. Their visual impact never ceases to excite one's senses; they change from regal to whimsical, from utterly bold to exquisitely subtle. Secondly, each rug has a story to tell. Tibetans are passionate traders. Salesmanship and negotiation skills are highly regarded and relished as a national pastime by all participants, including bystanders. Since rugs are so treasured, even the most mundane old rug often comes with fantastic stories of provenance and importance as expounded by the seller.

It is through collecting that my admiration for the Tibetan weavers and my involvement with their craft deepened. In 1986, I returned to my homeland from the United States to explore the possibility of producing a collection of traditional Tibetan carpets in Tibet that could meet the standards of discerning collectors.

I returned to New York from my trip with the realization that although the challenges involved in operating a successful rug-weaving enterprise in Tibet were daunting, they could and must be overcome. I simply could not accept that Tibet, with its glorious rug-weaving heritage, abundance of the highland sheep wool, and large population of weavers and artisans, would remain unable to enter the international market. I was convinced that the success of such an enterprise would mean not only a revitalized Tibetan rug-weaving heritage, but also livelihood for significant numbers of Tibetans in their homeland.

The challenge of this project became irresistible to me.

In the production process that begun in 1987, I worked closely with a number of master weavers whose depth of knowledge of the craft was most impressive. I realized that the wonderful tales of their craft, transmitted orally by their teachers, who in turn learned from their teachers before them, was an intrinsic part of Tibet's rug-weaving heritage. I felt compelled to celebrate their craft. Thus I conceived the idea for this book.

I was fortunate to have Trinley Chodrak as my co-author. His wealth of knowledge of Tibetan cultural history was vital in realizing our objective for the book—that of discussing the evolutionary development of Tibetan rugs in the context of Tibetan geography, culture, and society. Lincoln Potter's photography eloquently captures the visual images of Tibetan nomads, weavers, and artisans in the context of Tibetan terrain and cultural landscape.

Finally, I am delighted that it is Hallvard Kuløy, author of *Tibetan Rugs*, one of the earliest books on the subject, who is introducing and publishing this book. In 1982, when Tibet was still closed to outside travelers, Hal observed in his book that: "original material on Tibetan rug making tradition is rapidly disappearing, and it is important that one now starts in earnest to recover and preserve this marvelous art."

Hal's book has been an important companion to me throughout these last twelve years of collecting, producing, and now writing. Our shared passion for Tibetan rugs and the importance of their heritage has generated the dynamics to set the looms in motion again in Tibet.

I am grateful to the very many people who shared their passion in and knowledge of rugs with me. The old masters who told me the tales of their craft, and the others who sold me rugs often relishing each transaction with wonderful tales of their rugs, are too numerous to name here. But their generosity has made this book possible. I ask them to share whatever merit this book offers. I alone must accept responsibility for any error or shortcomings of its content.

Kesang G. Tashi

14

Festivities under an
appliqué tent.

The Tibetan saying *mi chig la den chig,* or "a carpet for every person," will not evince the slightest surprise from anyone who has set foot in a Tibetan home. Indeed, carpets may outnumber people in many Tibetan dwellings. One of the most essential and prized items for the peasant, nomad, monk, or aristocrat, the Tibetan woolen rug, notably a *khaden* or "three-by-six," is possibly the single cultural artifact capable of gracing the adobe-floored room or yak-hair tent, warming the heart and souls of those sturdy folk inhabiting the vast grasslands of the Tibetan northern plains, where temperatures drop well below zero, or the fertile river valleys of the south and east.

The Tibetan carpet was accorded special symbolic value in Tibetan society from early times. In the fourteenth-century biography of the pre-eminent yogi and Tibetan cultural hero, Mila Repa (A.D. 1040–1123), for instance, the poet-saint visits his spiritual guru Marpa, whom he finds seated on a knotted-pile rug *drumtse:* "(Marpa was) seated on top of two layers of cushion and a carpet *(drumtse),* making three layers, over a floor carpet *(sap-den)."* (*Tsang Nyong,* fifteenth century text)

Likewise, reference is made to the knotted-pile rug drumtse in a biography of the great lama Dromton (A.D. 1004–1064) about a noted patron of religious practitioners presenting the lama a carpet as a gesture of respect: "While Dromton was on a journey from Kham to Western Tibet, he met a great man called Trankha Bherchung near the river Sokchu. Bherchung was so moved by Dromton's teachings that he rose and rolled up the drumtse from under his buttocks and offered it to the learned priest in homage." (*Pawo,* sixteenth century text)

The bestowing of this kind of status to carpet use did not develop overnight in Tibet. In all likelihood, a range of rugs was commonly used by every social group when these works were written, if not much earlier. References to *den,* the generic Tibetan term for carpet, seat, or cushion, occur in Tibetan texts of the seventh century. According to at least one later source, den were used at the Tibetan king's court in the seventh century (Stein, 1992). This was a significant time in Tibetan history as it marked the introduction of the entrenchment of Buddhism in Tibet, and the invention of the Tibetan script. The recording of Tibetan history began then as well. Thus, Tibetan carpets are at least as old as Tibetan literature itself.

ORIGINS OF THE CRAFT

As to the origins of Tibetan rug weaving, the craft most likely evolved indigenously and in isolation. This explains the unique weaving technique and the physical structure of Tibetan rugs and reinforces the notion that Tibetan rug weaving

A

BRIEF

HISTORY

OF

TIBETAN

TEXTILES

AND

CARPETS

Opposite: Picnic with a view of the Potala.

was distinct from that of neighboring India and China, as well as from other extant weaving traditions worldwide, with the sole exception, curiously, of the Scandinavian *rya* rug, which is similar in its construction as early Tibetan cut-loop weaving methods. (Denwood, 1974)

Specifically, it was the use of the archaic vertical loom and the method of mounting the warp on the loom that were uniquely Tibetan. Subsequently, the Tibetan tradition absorbed influences from Turkestan in the north, India in the south and west, and more recently, design elements from China in the east. The result was a fusion of indigenous textile weaving influenced by the techniques of many neighboring cultures.

Originally a utilitarian household craft, both textile weaving and carpet weaving evolved out of the need for protection against the harsh environment of the high plateau. The early nomadic hunting tribes of Tibet could not have survived without knowing rudimentary methods of weaving textiles for making garments and tents. These early textile-weaving techniques improved over the centuries, far beyond the crude fabrics used for protection, to become textiles that were increasingly complex in structure and decorative in color and design.

EARLY TIBETAN CIVILIZATION

That such tribes inhabited the vast expanses on the roof of the world since earliest times is proven by archaeological findings. Excavations at the site of Karo village near Chamdo and a site near Lhasa have unearthed evidence of Neolithic settlements in the river valleys of eastern and central Tibet between 3100 and 3600 B.C. Findings include remains of dwelling foundations, pottery, tools, bone ornaments, as well as signs of agriculture. Stone tools excavated in the western Tsang and northwestern Chang Thang regions date to 8,000 years ago. (Hou, 1990)

It is generally accepted that by the beginning of the Christian era, tribes had settled in the Yarlung valley of southern Tibet on the banks of the Tsangpo (Brahmaputra) River. These were the semi-nomadic agriculturalists and pastoralists who occupied parts of India, Nepal, China, and Turkestan in the seventh to ninth centuries, at the height of Tibet's military expansion. The discovery of Tibetan texts from the eighth to ninth centuries at Dunhuang, a "Silk Road" oasis controlled by the Yarlung rulers from A.D. 787 to 848, provide the earliest glimpse of these kings and their subjects. Although the chronology of reigns prior to A.D. 500 is sketchy, later accounts of the same kings paint a credible portrait of society in southern Tibet.

Gyantse master weaver
Gyen Yonten La.

Several accounts regarding the life of the near-mythical first Yarlung king, Nyatri Tsenpo, indicate that livestock were being domesticated during or before his reign. In the most plausible chronology of the period, the sixteenth century historian Pawo Tsuk puts Nyatri Tsenpo's reign at 360–300 B.C. There are detailed accounts of the advances made in material culture from seven generations after Nyatri Tsenpo, during the reign of the eighth king, Pude Kungyel. One such source is exemplary:

"Po Rgod Bya Rkhri, the able hero, maneuvered rivers to flow into fields and turned forests into fertile lands…nomads lived in the highlands and farmers in the valleys. He organized youth defense and the mining of silver, copper, and iron to be made into implements. The old and able educated the young in various skills and gave advice to their subjects; stone carving, masonry and carpentry were practiced." (*Pawo Tsukla,* sixteenth-century text)

The first literary references to wool-craft also date to the same period, from between the first centuries B.C. and A.D. In the chronicle cited above, an old yarn-spinning lady is credited with compiling a prototype of the Tibetan lunar calendar, suggesting the presence of woolen textile-weaving activity during the king's reign. In light of the level of social evolution reached in Yarlung during this time, which was probably comparable throughout central and southern Tibet, we should not be surprised to find that yarn spinning and some form of textile production existed.

Doma Chodun discussing rug design.

The first conclusive evidence of a textile-weaving tradition occurs only 600 years later, with the extensive military campaigns of Tibet's first Buddhist king, Songtsen Gampo (A.D.617–650). Chinese annals from the Tang dynasty describe Songtsen Gampo's army passing by or camping in what is today the Chinese province of Gansu: "Below the Wongtho region of Drugu, the Tibetan army set up black tent encampments on their journeys." (*New Tang Annals*)

Woven from dark yak hair, Tibetan nomad tents remain black to this day, suggesting this indigenous textile weaving tradition has been preserved by Tibetan nomads for more than 1,300 years. What enabled the yak-hair tent to withstand the severe conditions of the plateau are the intrinsic properties of yak hair and a tent-weaving tradition that predated Songtsen Gampo's army by several centuries, at least to the time of Pude Kunggyel's reign over Yarlung valley at the turn of the millennium.

Today, Tibetan herds not only produce yak hair and sheep wool but goat hair (*ra-pu*), goat cashmere (*ra-kulu*), and yak cashmere (*yak-kulu*). Every wool and hair fiber of these animals is used for weaving except for goat cashmere, which enjoys a high market value and is thus exported. Besides its use in making tent fabric, ropes, slings, and bags, yak hair was also woven into ornamental textiles to protect against the malevolent elements at the entrances of monastery buildings. The same archaic technique is used in weaving yak cashmere and wool blankets and in making bags of wool, goat hair, and yak hair. Since we can assume that these herds produced more sheep wool than any other fiber, it is probable that woolen flat-weaves of the same construction (*liwu*) were made simultaneously, as they are today, with yak-hair textiles (*dzipa*).

The same technique of construction is used in weaving dzipa and liwu. First, yarn is spun into thick strands that provide the wefts and warps; the warp threads are then strung around a back-strap loom (*pangthag*) that rests either on the weaver's lap or a horizontal frame-loom. One would guess the back-strap loom to be eminently suited to nomadic lifestyle as it only consists of a few pieces of wood, a strap that is tied around the weaver's waist, and stones or pegs to keep the loom stable, while the upright horizontal loom was probably the innovation of more sedentary semi-nomads. On both types of looms, yarn is passed from side to side through the warps to produce a narrow strip of flat-woven fabric, usually between 10 to 16 inches wide. The strips are sewn together to make the fabric for a tent, bag, or blanket. Whereas tent textiles are typically in natural black-brown in color with no design, bags and blankets often carry simple stripes, which is achieved by alternating dyed yarn with natural white, gray, beige, and brown yarns. Woolen liwu is commonly woven by non-nomadic villagers today, but the origin of this flat-weave technique is indisputably linked to and probably an evolution of the ancient flat-weave that nomads used for making their tents.

EARLY GARMENT TEXTILES

By the seventh century A.D. the Tibetan king and his court were wearing ornate Persian-style robes of apparently complex form, judging from their depiction in early wall paintings and eighth and ninth century sculptures. The most vivid of these early portrayals is a seventh century Chinese painting of Songtsen Gampo's minister, Gar Tongtsen, at the Tang court in Chang'an, where he went to claim and win, as some believe, a Chinese princess on behalf of the Tibetan king. The Tibetan minister is wearing a long robe decorated with medallions that seems to have been fashionable throughout the Persian Sassanid Empire from the third to seventh centuries. At its height, Sassanian artistic and material culture spread throughout Kashmir and Central Asia and as far east as China. Ancient sculptures of bodhisattvas clothed in the same medallion robes have survived in Tibet at a temple called Yemar near Gyantse. In the sculpted images of eighth and ninth centuries at the Potala in Lhasa, Songtsen Gampo and his two queens appear to be wearing Persian-style long robes. Thus, quite possibly, Tibetans were using, if not producing, finely woven garment textiles at the time.

According to the *White Annals,* a Tibetan text based on older sources now lost, Minister Gar arrived at the Tang court and was struck by the brilliantly colored, fine silk garments worn by the Chinese officials, and was humbled that the Tibetans only had simple *nambu* clothing. This would mean that by the mid-seventh century, ordinary Tibetan clothing was made of finely woven nambu, the quintessential Tibetan textile, while members of the royal entourage favored more elaborate attire modeled on Persian robes then in vogue throughout Central Asia. The Tibetan term *chuba* for the traditional full-length over-garment, commonly made of nambu, suggests an ancient connection to the Persian dress, for in both colloquial and literary Tibetan chuba is curiously close to *juba,* the Turkish word-denoting robe. (Laufer, 1918:86)

It seems certain nambu was being woven during Songtsen Gampo's reign, given the similarity of techniques used in making nambu twill fabric and yak-hair flat-weaves (dzipa) used in making Tibetan tents. The construction of nambu and dzipa is virtually identical. The only technical distinction is that two heddles are added in weaving nambu so that there are four instead of two sheds. Nambu is thus constructed on four separate finely spun wool warps, which allows it to achieve a

Checking the yarn color
at the Gyantse workshop.

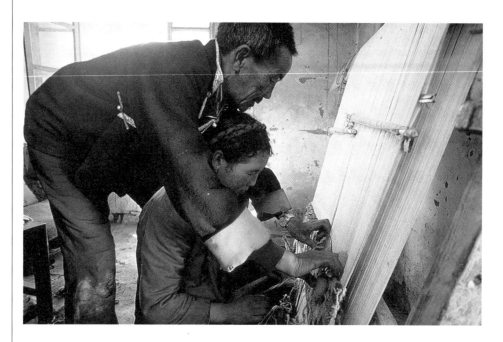

denser, smoother fabric than the coarser dzipa. By contrast, the yak-hair dzipa is constructed on only two separate wefts from a much thicker yarn that results in a looser weave.

Such improvements in textile-weaving techniques was possible partly due to the advent of skilled wool-yarn spinning, which existed in a simpler form much earlier. Further refinement in yarn production led to the development of fine sherma serge fabric and the traditional Tibetan apron textile *pangden,* woven by the same technique as in making nambu though with even finer yarn. It was the introduction of the horizontal frame loom among Tibet's sedentary and semi-nomadic population, however, that was key to the development of nambu twill and these finer fabrics. More stable than the simple back-strap apparatus, the frame loom provided the weaving tension necessary to producing a tighter, denser, more finely woven textile.

"PLANTED-PILE" TEXTILES AND THE EVOLUTION OF DRUMTSE
While these innovations brought about the refinement of nambu, the simple dzipa and liwu flat-weaves were being modified to produce the woolen *tsukdruk,* or "planted-pile" textile, also called *treche,* meaning "knife-cut" in Tibetan. Still widely used in Tibet to make bulky garments and thick blankets, tsukdruk is woven on both back-strap and horizontal frame looms and produced in the same narrow strips as liwu and dzipa. The planted-pile weave is created by looping a weft yarn around a thin metal rod while pulling it through the warp. The loops are cut by passing a knife blade or

The master teaches weaving techniques.

24

fingernail along the rod, which results in a row of unknotted pile with each cut loop held to the textile by one or more warp threads. Tsukdruk fabric is woven by using two or four sheds, depending on the quality desired; a double weft is pulled through the warps last, and the row of pile tightened by beating with a wooden hammer.

The same planted-pile technique was used to weave the first Tibetan pile rug, the primitive *tsukden,* which literally means "planted-pile rug." Still woven today by farmers and nomads, the tsukden pile rug differs from the tsukdruk textile in yarn proportion and density; otherwise the two weaving techniques are identical. In light of the close structural similarities of the archaic yak-hair textile (dzipa), wool blanket flat-weave (liwu), twill garment fabric (nambu), and planted-pile textile (tsukdruk), the direct connection between early carpets and ancient nomadic textile weaving becomes clear. This link is also reflected in the terminology: *tsuk,* the syllable denoting the verb "to plant in," distinguishes the tsukdruk textile from its pile-less precursor namdruk (colloquially, nambu). The same weaving technique was used in making a pile carpet rather than a textile, so the term became tsukden, or "planted-pile rug," suggesting these ancient traditions evolved concurrently, sharing technology and materials from their earliest stages of development.

Drumtse, The Classic Tibetan Pile Carpet

That the Tibetan planted pile carpet tsukden and related textiles go back to antiquity should not be surprising. The nature of rural Tibetan life in antiquity or at the turn of the century was not significantly different, and Tibetans were isolated from the modern world until recently. Even today, in much of the countryside the principal occupations of farming and livestock breeding continue much as they have done for centuries: the sedentary population grew barley and other crops in the warm months and engaged in wool-craft and brewing barley beer (*chang*) during the long winters. Much as before, nomadic pastoralists come to the farming valleys with meat, wool, and other livestock products, which they trade for grain and other goods. This basic pattern of life has remained essentially unchanged since the beginning of Tibet's recorded history, and Tibetan weaving traditions may have remained similarly intact over a comparable period.

If tsukden, the primitive planted-pile carpet, and related textiles go back to antiquity, however, when did the more advanced pile carpet drumtse develop? Woven on stationary upright vertical looms, drumtse employs an archaic method of tying multiple yarn knots around a continuous warp thread. This only survives in contemporary Tibet though it may have been common in antiquity. The knotted pile of drumtse is better fastened to the warp structure than the planted pile of tsukden, and drumtse weaving technique produces more elaborate designs and a finer uniform texture. Whereas tsukden designs are typically limited to simple geometric patterns or solid field designs rendered in one or two colors, drumtse often displays more complex pictorial, geometric, and abstract designs in a wide range of colors.

According to Tibetan oral tradition, drumtse came after tsukden, which is used today not only by nomads and semi-nomadic farmer-nomads (*samadrok*) but by farming households that cannot afford the more prized drumtse. Requiring far less wood, the horizontal frames and back-strap looms used to weave tsukden are portable and cost less to construct. The upright vertical loom on which drumtse is woven is bulkier and rarely transported. Clearly, the heavy vertical loom belongs to a more sedentary culture just as drumtse weaving, with its technical and aesthetic refinements, is the product of a more developed and stratified society. Thus, we see how drumtse naturally evolved from its simple precursors, the tsukden, nambu, and liwu wool-weaving traditions.

Wangden Drumtse and Kamdrum

One fascinating oral tradition suggests that the technical link between the primitive tsukden and the fully developed, knotted drumtse may have been provided by the "Wangden drumste" or "Wangden," a cruder version of the knotted-pile rug still woven in some villages of the Wangden valley in Tsang province. Wangden resembles the tsukden and other "planted-pile" textiles in pile length, density, and yarn thickness, but Wangden carpets are woven on the same upright vertical looms used in weaving the classical drumtse carpet. Though the technique of mounting the continuous warp in Wangden drumtse is identical to that used in drumtse weaving, the knotting is simpler and produces pile less securely knotted to the warp.

As with both drumtse and tsukden, the pile yarn of Wangden drumtse is looped around an iron rod and cut to make the pile, which is held to the rug by warp threads. But if the unknotted pile of tsukden is precariously looped around the warp threads, and the drumtse pile is securely knotted to them, the Wangden pile falls somewhere in between. Loosely pulled around parallel pairs of front facing or "top face" warps, Wangden carpet pile is only slightly better secured to the rug than tsukden pile. The result is the distinctive "warp back-face" of the Wangden, since the pile is only tied around warp threads located at the face of the rug. By contrast, drumtse knots are simultaneously tied to warps at both the face and back of the rug, binding them more tightly and securely.

While many antique drumtse incorporate a creative and eclectic multitude of half, quarter, and insert knots, which were employed by skilled weavers to render intricate designs and to compensate for relatively low knottage, contemporary drumtse typically use only the standard full Tibetan knot. Interestingly, many of the insert knots found in antique drumtse are identical in construction to those of the planted-pile tsukden even though, in the latter, they are not actually knotted but loosely held to the rug by just one or two warps. The full drumtse knot, on the other hand, is virtually identical in shape and construction to the standard Wangden knot. The difference is that the drumtse knot is securely tied around two front-facing and two back-facing warps, whereas the Wangden knot is more precariously tied around two pairs of front-facing warps. The fact that drumtse weaving incorporates techniques of tsukden and Wangden weaving suggest that these primitive pile-weaving traditions preceded drumtse and were instrumental in the development of drumtse into a more complex and secure rug.

Similarly, the traditional long-piled borders (*ring-pu*) of Wangden rugs are identical to the unknotted pile of tsukden, suggesting that the Wangden carpet may have represented an early improvement of the planted-pile tsukden. According to an oral tradition cited by former weavers of the Wangden valley, Wangden carpets existed "long before" drumste, which they believe was first woven in Kampa Dzong, a town not far and southwest of Wangden valley towards the former country of Sikkim. Indeed, it is a common belief that drumtse originated in Kampa Dzong in all the traditionally prominent weaving villages of Tsang province, including Gyantse, Gabshi, Drongtse, Changra, and Shigatse. Throughout the once-prosperous carpet-weaving belt, in which someone in every household knew how to weave drumtse, the colloquial Kam-drum, an abbreviation of "Kampa Dzong drumtse," becomes the pedantic "drumtse." In Kampa Dzong itself, however, drumtse weaving has long since declined and the town no longer produces pile carpets of any distinction.

The Wangden Story

Wangden Valley, which consists of twenty villages and three monasteries, is located in Tsang province, south of Penam Dzong on the main road between Gyantse and Shigatse. It is said the people of Wangden descended from five nomad families that settled in the valley ten centuries ago. They believe the Wangden rug weaving technique originated in the two villages of Bushar and Bunup at the southern end of the valley. It was here that the five families first settled and where the valley's oldest monastery, no longer functioning, stands. Today, many of the valley inhabi-

Showing off the Gyantse
production.

tants describe themselves as farmer-nomads (*samadrok*), practicing both animal husbandry and agriculture, and nomad camps at higher elevations around the southern end of the valley to the south, west, and east.

According to legend, the weaving of Wangden "warp back-face" rugs began when a revered lama from the monastery, Jamyang Tame Gyentsen, wove a square meditation pile rug with a medallion design that inspired villagers to follow his example. Initially, the villagers only copied the medallion design, but following the lama's death, they discovered a text he had composed. The text supposedly contained drawings of Buddhist symbols and other design elements deemed appropriate for representation in Wangden carpets and was accompanied by instructions on color usage as well as other guidelines. Although the text subsequently disappeared, weavers from the same two villages to this day observe a strict code of weaving that governs design, coloration, proportion, and knot count, which, we are to believe, was passed down from one generation to the other, beginning with the revered lama.

Under Jamyang Gyentsen's influence, goes the legend, Wangden carpets won a new patron, the Gelugpa, or "Yellow Hat" sect of Tibetan Buddhism. It is said women were prohibited from weaving Wangden intended for ecclesiastical use, as decreed by the Dalai Lama himself. Wangden carpets were regularly commissioned for the Potala Palace and for "big three" Gelugpa monasteries of Drepung, Sera, and Ganden, and a full set of new monastic runners and sitting carpets was made every year for the New Year Monlam Prayer Festival at Lhasa's Jokhang Temple. The illustrious Tsongkhapa (1357–1419), the founder of the Gelugpa sect, the Great Fifth Dalai Lama (1617–82), and many Gelugpa lamas are said to have used Wangden carpets while meditating.

There is no doubt Wangden carpets were widely used in monasteries throughout Tibet: antique Wangden runners can still be seen in the assembly halls of most monasteries in central Tibet. Also, early twentieth century travelers brought back photographs of Wangden rugs on monastery thrones and sitting cushions as far away from Wangden Valley as Ladakh to the far west, and Amdo to the far northeast. Be that as it may, it seems inconclusive, and even spurious, that the lama Jamyang Gyentsen Tame invented the Wangden or the Wangden prototype. At the most, he might have helped to popularize and raise the status of an existing weaving tradition, probably by inspiring a Buddhist code of design, color, and structural symbolism that won Gelugpa patronage and that survives today. This historical revisionism may be attributed to the fact that Wangden Valley converted to the Gelugpa school in the seventeenth century, even though the weaving technique dates to long before the first five nomad families settled in the south of Wangden Valley, possibly predating the valley's folklore by several centuries.

The Warp-Back Rugs of Lhuntse Dzong

There is yet another challenge to the Wangden claim. For though the people of Wangden valley maintain that Wangden carpets were made only in their valley, pile rugs of identical construction were being woven in Lhuntse, far to the southeast in Lhoka district, up to the early 1950s. The design and materials of the "Wangden drumtse" of Lhuntse are distinct from that of Wangden Valley: with few exceptions, the antique designs of the Wangden drumtse consist of large yellow, red, and blue yungdrung, or swastikas, on a dark brown field of yak cashmere pile with no border. The rare non-swastika designs with a border are archaic and suggest Turkestani influence. At any rate, none resembles the designs attributed to the lama Jamyang Tame Gyentsen.

It is interesting to note that goat and yak outnumber sheep in Lhuntse which, like Wangden, is inhabited by *samadrok* claiming a nomadic ancestry. Scarcity of sheep wool is what led Lhuntse weavers to use dark yak cashmere as a source of pile yarn where possible and they used goat and yak hair for warps, wefts, and long fringes (*ring-pu*) at the edge of their rugs. Unlike the rugs of Wangden Valley, which enjoyed wide popularity throughout Tibet, probably prompted by religious patronage, Lhuntse's rugs were woven mainly for local needs—households and a few monasteries nearby. Despite the neglect suffered by the Wangden drumtse weaving tradition in recent decades, weavers in Lhuntse today faithfully replicate the old swastika rugs in design and proportion, employing the classic Kamdrum drumtse technique. They use black wool yarn available in the market and cotton yarn for warps and wefts.

This development probably occurred throughout southern Tibet over several centuries as the Kamdrum drumtse gained popularity and the use of Wangden drumtse declined. Structurally more secure and capable of producing elaborate designs, the popular preference for Kamdrum would have ensured the gradual replacement of Wangden rugs almost everywhere. As Kamdrum gained prominence, Wangden drumtse weaving was gradually reduced to a small Gelug-patronized activity in Wangden Valley, though it survives in isolated places like Lhuntse. The survival of the craft in Lhuntse is explained partly by the relative scarcity of wool in the region, which in turn perpetuated the use of goat and yak hair warps, yak cashmere pile, and the archaic technique of Wangden weaving.

Influence From Neighboring Regions

Both the classical Kampadzong drumtse and the more primitive Wangden drumtse are woven on the Tibetan vertical loom identified as an ancient model of Turkish or Caucasian origin. It predates the Persian and Tabriz models imported from the Middle East by India and China. (Denwood 1974:90) The Tibetan method of mounting the warp continuously on the loom and the cut-loop knotted pile of both Wangden and Kamdrum rugs are found nowhere else. It clearly sets apart Tibetan rug weaving from the rug weaving of India and China. It is generally accepted that the latter's more sophisticated looms and weaving techniques were imported via the Middle East in recent centuries, whereas the Tibetan loom and knotting technique are indigenous and of a much earlier origin.

This significantly disproves a notion, held even by some Tibetans, that rug weaving was introduced to Tibet by King Songtsen Gampo's Chinese princess in the seventh century. This is clearly erroneous. There is no evidence of carpet weaving in China before the fifteenth to sixteenth centuries, and the visible Chinese design influences in many Tibetan rugs simply reflects of the Tibetan predilection for Chinese textiles and porcelain.

For that matter, Tibetan carpets carry influences of Khotanese and other Turkish design elements, underlining the long cultural connection between Tibet and East Turkestan. These ties are at least as old as Tibetan Buddhism, and they have existed uninterrupted ever since Songtsen Gampo's army occupied the Taklamakan desert oases of Kashgar and Khotan in the seventh century. The Chinese Buddhist pilgrim Xuan Zang observed carpet production in these Silk Road oases in the seventh century. It is almost certain the craft was practiced there

Trimming and carving the rug.

Hand carding the wool
before spinning into yarn.

much earlier. At the time of his visit, Khotan was the religious and artistic center of the entire Tarim Basin, supporting more than five thousand Buddhist monks and a hundred monasteries. The legacy of Khotanese artisans and architects invited to Tibet in the eighth and ninth centuries survives in the sculpted images found in the Yarlung and Lhasa valleys; the influence of Khotanese and Central Asian idioms on later Tibetan art is also evident throughout central Tibet.

It is quite possible Khotanese carpet weavers came to Tibet during this period of its military expansion and cultural exchanges. The modern Tibetan historian Shakabpa suggests that Khotanese monks were present at the Tibetan court as early as the mid-ninth century, during the reign of the Yarlung king Ralpachen: "In the year 841 A.D., the Iron Bird Year, Liyul Warkhen of Yarkand, Khotan, on the invitation of the Tibetans, sent expert craftsmen to Tibet. They contributed to the improvement of weaving in Tibet."

In this regard, a number of ancient rug fragments that appeared at the turn of the century are of particular interest. Discovered in Khotan and at two other Silk Road oases, they date from the second to fourth centuries A.D. The construction of some of these fragments closely resemble that of drumtse, suggesting that the cut-loop knotting technique in weaving drumtse may date to Songtsen Gampo's occupation of Khotan, if not to earlier cultural contact. Fragments of comparable age excavated in Syria and Egypt are also of a similar construction, suggesting a continuum of weaving culture emanating from the Persian Sassanid Empire, which at its height bordered the Taklamakan desert and its carpet-producing oases. (Denwood 1974:84,92)

There is an alternative or perhaps concurrent route by which foreign influence may have traveled—through Kashmir. An obscure Tibetan oral tradition ascribes an early source of technical innovation to the *la-drum,* the Ladakhi pile rug. Given that there is no known history of vertical rug-weaving looms in Ladakh, however, this could be a reference to the arrival in Tibet of rugs from the West. They would have come presumably via the Silk Road oases to the north of Ladakh, or through nearby Kashmir, both strongly influenced by Sassanian culture as late as the sixth to seventh centuries.

Whether the first Tibetan drumtse was woven by a farmer, lama, or court artisan, surely the range of practical functions that carpets came to serve for every social group is what ensured the craft's survival through the centuries. Fittingly, Tibetans of all stations placed great value on their carpets, whether a pair of ceremonial sitting rugs unrolled only for occasions such as the Losar, the Tibetan New Year, or a simple back-strap tsukden with few colors and little design, carried by yak from pasture to pasture for a nomad to sleep on in his tent.

Tibetan rug weaving thus evolved indigenously. Carpets were woven first and foremost for home use, and then for sale in the market or as a gift for a monastery. The technique of weaving was handed down from one generation to another as an important practical skill, much in the way textile weaving techniques were passed down. The supreme utility of the Tibetan carpet may explain how such an archaic weaving method endured so long, more than an estimated thousand years, despite the arrival of more advanced technology from China, India, Persia, and Turkestan, all neighbors with which Tibet had regular contact throughout its history.

Unlike the more elaborate weaving traditions of these countries, which catered predominantly to the tastes of royal courts and later to foreign markets, Tibetan carpets were made almost exclusively for Tibetans. Not surprisingly, the result was a rich and vibrant folk-art tradition, shaped by an indigenous aesthetic that was unmistakably and delightfully Tibetan.

EMERGENCE OF GYANTSE AS TIBET'S RUG WEAVING CENTER

It is well known that the best and greatest quantity of carpets in Tibet came from the southern region of Tsang. True for centuries, the Tsang region still has the highest concentration of weavers in Tibet. In the words of the late master carpet weaver Mingmar Wangdui, when he was a young man in the 1930s, "every family in Gyantse owned at least one loom" for carpet weaving. Today, Gyantse remains the most prominent weaving town in Tsang, a position it enjoyed from the fifteenth century, judging from a historical text of that period, *Nyang Chochung:* "In the upper region (Gyatso) there was a big market convention, with two tribes, and three large nomad centers. The people traded in felt hats, yak tails, and nambu . . . In the middle region (Gyantse), there was a big bazaar, with two tribes. The people traded in yak hair textiles, drumtse, and felt."(*Pawo,* sixteenth-century text)

Strategically located on the main Lhasa-Sikkim trade route in a fertile farming valley, Gyantse was affluent enough for each family to afford to weave rugs for its

CARPET
WEAVING
AS A
COMMERCIAL
ENTERPRISE
IN TIBET

Opposite: Changthang nomads at the Naqu horse festival.

own use and had surplus to sell or barter. The weaving community created a local "carpet culture" unique to Gyantse and its satellite villages, sharing new designs and technical innovations. Similarly, weaving centers in other parts of Tsang such as Shigatse, Drongtse, and Gabshi developed their own provincial aesthetics, distinct from one another, though often linked by parallel influences and shared tastes.

For example, designs derived from Chinese silk brocade became very fashionable in Gyantse in the early twentieth century, reflecting the tastes of the nobility in Tsang and Lhasa. At the same time, the use of wool warps went out of vogue, following the introduction of cotton yarn by the wife of David MacDonald, the British trade agent stationed in Gyantse in the 1920s. The Gabshi weaving center, however, did not use cotton yarn for warps until the late 1950s, and Drongtse in the 1930s was producing all-wool rugs with designs that had been popular in the late nineteenth century. Meanwhile, in Lhasa, designs introduced by the aristocrat Kapshopa in the early twentieth century, known as "Kapshopa's new designs," had become immensely popular and were being copied widely.

Notwithstanding such provincial variations in design and taste, rug weaving was never subjected to the strict conventions imposed on religious art and some other crafts because carpets were produced primarily for household or other practical uses. The widespread home production of carpets for private use resulted in an almost infinite variation of design and color combination that nonetheless was distinctly Tibetan in character. In retrospect, they represent by far the freest, most expressive and variegated body of Tibetan folk art.

Increased Domestic Demand for Carpets

Curiously, there was only sporadic trading in carpets between Tibet and its immediate neighbors to the south, even though the busy Lhasa-Sikkim trade route passed through Tibet's most prominent weaving region. Except for a small market in the Indian Himalaya for Tibetan saddle carpets (as well as flat-weave liwu blankets), the only known demand for Tibetan carpets from the south prior to the turn of the century came from the Newars of Kathmandu, who used long, narrow runners at wedding ceremonies and special feasting occasions.

Rather, the principal market for Tibetan carpets was always within Tibet. Originally made at home for home use and for barter, the demand for carpets rose as carpet use spread to areas where rug weaving was not so prevalent as in Gyantse and other parts of Tsang. Valued for their function and their decorative use, carpets gradually came to be regarded as essential household items. It soon became unthinkable for even a humble Tibetan family to be without at least one good pair of bed-size rugs.

The prevalent use of carpets in monasteries also played an important role in their development. References to carpets in biographies of religious personages suggest that an early use of rugs was as meditation seats. According to oral tradition, some of Tibet's most distinguished religious figures used khagangma sitting rugs, including the fourteenth century scholar-saint Tsongkhapa, whose teachings became the basis of the Gelugpa sect of Tibetan Buddhism. As monasteries grew in wealth and power in Tibet, there was an enormous demand for rugs of all sizes and shapes.

The Rise of Commercial Weaving Centers

With the domestic demand for carpets rising, trading in carpets became lucrative, and rug production became established as a commercial enterprise. By the late nineteenth century, several estates in and around Gyantse were employing weavers and wool workers at organized workshops, as observed by travelers like Sarat Chandra Das and Perceval Landon. Just when these estate-run workshops first came about is uncertain, but what is known is that the Chinese weaving center of Ningxia was producing temple runners with snow lion medallion designs for Tibetan monasteries as early as the seventeenth century. Since Tibetan weavers would have supplied the greater share of the monastic demand for temple runners, square khagangma, and other rugs, organized estate workshops of the kind observed in the nineteenth century presumably sprang up at the same time, if not earlier, as the production of Ningxia carpets for Tibet's wealthy monasteries.

Pair of tiger design *bokcha* rugs flank an entrance in the Norbulingka.

Conservative and traditional until the mid-twentieth century, the social customs of Tibet in the 1920s were probably little changed from what prevailed hundreds of years earlier. According to Jigme Taring, a member of a formerly aristocratic family whose estate in Lhasa produced carpets in the 1920s and 1930s, most aristocratic estates owned at least one loom and kept weavers on the estate premises, producing a large quantity of high quality carpets each year for the estate's own use as well as for gifts and offerings to monasteries. Besides rug weavers, the Taring estate in Lhasa employed textile weavers, wool workers, furniture-makers and tailors.

Typically, estates recruited village weavers to work in lieu of paying grain tax, though they provided them food and clothing, and allowed weavers to work at their own pace. At the Taring estate, wool workers were given a daily ration of *tsampa* (roasted barley flour) and *thukpa* (Tibetan noodle soup) of three varieties, in accordance with their skill; rug weavers and seamstresses were ranked as the second grade. The meat of an entire sheep could be the reward for a weaving job well done, while workers who were slow or not up to the mark were sent back to the fields and replacements found for them. The estate workers were permitted to weave their own carpets in the evenings, and these they generally sold at the local market.

With the proliferation of such small-scale estate production throughout central and southern Tibet, some enterprising aristocrats and wealthy trading families began setting up commercial workshops. By the early twentieth century, the most prominent of these were the Gyantse estates of the Phala and Langdong nobility,

Liwu flat-weave and *Tsukdruk* blankets on display for sale.

and two other estates in the nearby villages of Gabshi and Changra. Largest of these, the Gabshi workshop in the late 1940s employed fifty rug and textile weavers, yarn spinners, and other wool-craft workers, including two master carpet weavers. These craft workers were villagers who were paid in tsampa and any wool they could discreetly take home. Out of these employees, fourteen were carpet weavers, each weaving about fifteen rugs a year, mostly bed-size carpets, cushion covers, saddle rugs and other ornamental horse trappings for sale on the market but also customized order of throne back-rests and large floor carpets. According to oral history cited by former estate weavers, the Gabshi estate's rug weaving enterprise dates to the planting of a peach tree, which is said to be more than 240 years old.

In the late 1940s, bed-size carpets of moderate quality were being sold at the Gyantse and Lhasa markets for about 700 Tibetan *sang* each. They were also bartered for goods from India such as cloth, kerosene, sweets, and cigarettes. For these markets the Gabshi estate produced carpets that included designs such as medallions taken from silk brocade; *kati rimo,* a geometric design of Turkestani origin; pictorial designs of tigers, cranes, phoenixes, and dragons; and a popular floral design "twelve lotuses" (*pema chunyi*). Some Gabshi weavers also recalled weaving four large floor carpets with floral and bamboo designs between 1948 and 1959, three commissioned by the aristocrat Ngabo and one by a Chinese official. These floor coverings were woven in maximum sizes on ten-foot-wide wooden looms. This is an interesting detail. It implies that carpet production in the Tsang estates was more advanced than in Lhasa as, during the same period, the government guild workshop was still weaving large floor carpets in separate pieces on small looms.

Gabshi, Changra, and another carpet weaving estate near Gyantse were minor estates of Lhasa's Doring family, which ran a small workshop at its estate in Lhasa. The late master weaver Dorje Ngodup, who worked at the Changra estate, was recruited to the family's Lhasa estate in the late 1920s, where he wove carpets until the 1950s. According to his daughter, Dorji Ngodup was so naughty as a young weaver that he had to be monitored by a string tied to his earring at one end and to a parrot at the other. The most popular designs woven at the Doring's Lhasa estate in the 1920s and 1930s were three stylized floral patterns called *tranong* (small flowers), *kapsho* (Kapshopa's floral design, with three large lotuses inside an elaborate border), and *phende* (another stylized lotus flower design). Other commonly woven designs were medallions taken from brocade, "twelve lotuses," and pictorial designs of dragons and phoenixes.

According to former weavers, the Gyantse estates belonging to the noble Phala family and the trading family Langdong were almost identical in size and organization to the Gabshi estate. The Gyantse estate of Yabshi Phunkhang, another noble estate, was also reputed for its carpet production, though the production was principally for its own use. Similar carpet-weaving enterprises sprang up in Lhasa, notably at the Doring and Kapshopa estates, but none of these ever came close to touching Gyantse's reputation as the producer of Tibet's finest carpets.

In those days, Lhasa merchants would send their representatives on the eight-day journey to the Gyantse workshop by horseback to place orders, often taking detailed design and size specifications, and returned to the Lhasa market with the finished products by horse, mule, and yak caravan. According to Taring, the biggest customers of carpets at Lhasa's market were traders from the eastern Tibetan region of Kham, where carpet weaving was not widespread, though carpets were in demand for use in homes, monasteries, and as horseback trappings.

CARPET WEAVING GAINS OFFICIAL RECOGNITION

During the 1920s, the reign of the thirteenth Dalai Lama (1878–1933) may be regarded as the renaissance of rug weaving in Tibet. Recognizing the importance of the craft, the government established the first official weavers' guild, modeled on the official craft guilds organized for wood carvers, stone masons, coppersmiths, and other artisans. Directors of the guild were awarded the title *letsenpa;* a third-rank position in local government, and graduates of the guild workshop received the official designation "master weavers." The best of the latter were recruited to Lhasa by the thirteenth Dalai Lama to weave rugs for the new Chensey Palace, in the Norbulingka, the summer residence of the Dalai Lama, as well as the eastern section of the Potala, which was undergoing major renovation. During this period, Sonam Topgyal, the most renowned of the Gyantse guild master weavers, was appointed a fifth-rank official and designated "National Master Weaver." The two famous rugs he wove for the Dalai Lama are a small pile bag (*chaplug*) of about six inches square, an ornamental accoutrement designed to hold a ritual water vase, and a scallop-shaped throne back-rest with two phoenixes facing each other, which can still be seen in the Norbulingka.

Although most estate workshops employed more weavers than the Gyantse guild, the quality of weaving at the guild workshop was considered Tibet's best. This was because estate workshops produced carpets for merchants and for domestic and trade markets, whereas guild workshops produced carpets almost exclusively for monastic and official use. The late master weaver Wangdui, who

A nomadic woman
dressed in homespun garb.

Monk in the Jokhang
seated on a temple runner.

apprenticed at the guild workshop, recalls that the guild's biggest customers were the monasteries, followed by local officials and the government in Lhasa. He remembers a long temple runner with snow lion medallions on a golden yellow field that was to be a gift for Namgyal Monastery. The workshop produced common bed-size carpets for officials' homes, and long runners were ordered to cover and decorate secular meeting rooms and assembly halls.

In 1953 a weaving guild was established in Lhasa modeled on the Gyantse guild. Ten of the best weavers, including Wangdui, were taken from the original Gyantse guild. Artists from Lhasa's thangka painting guild were also recruited to undergo training in carpet design. At the new Lhasa workshop Wangdui wove both temple runners and floor carpets for the Potala and Norbulingka palaces, as well as a set of smaller rugs for the fourteenth Dalai Lama's personal use. There were also saddle and bed-size carpets woven, which were used during his pilgrimage to the sacred lake Lhamo Lhatso. Sample designs for these special carpets and others commissioned by the Lhasa government needed the formal approval of the Dalai Lama's own handicrafts department before weaving could begin.

Master Weavers and Apprenticeship

Every estate-run and government guild workshop had at least one master weaver in residence. Besides being highly experienced and skilled, the master weaver often possessed exceptional artistic talent. Like the masters of other traditional art forms, master carpet weavers were respected for their talent, sometimes locally and in a few cases throughout Tibet. To become a master of any traditional craft or art form required long study and dedication. It entailed undergoing apprenticeship, practice and accomplishment loosely modeled on that of Tibetan monastic study, and not unlike the system of craft apprenticeship that existed in feudal Europe.

Since the most skilled and respected master weavers were assigned to preside over government guilds and large estate workshops, securing a formal apprenticeship at these weaving centers was a significant achievement. Being accepted as an apprentice often meant a financial sacrifice. The peasant family lost one field hand for the planting and harvest seasons, and often the apprenticeship came with a price or, rather, gift tag, or social connections were needed for it to happen. But it was appreciated as an opportunity to acquire a practical skill that would bring in future income for the family, and securing an apprenticeship with a noted master also won social recognition. Although carpet weaving was not an occupation of status, highly skilled weavers were nonetheless awarded the respect due artisans.

Early Lessons of an Apprentice

An apprentice at carpet weaving estates and guild workshops typically lasted from five to six years, beginning at age thirteen or so. The first stage of a formal apprenticeship was devoted to learning the rudiments of wool yarn production. The apprentice was responsible for wool carding and for washing the raw wool chosen for spinning into yarn. After washing the wool in cold water and drying it in the sun, spiked wooden brushes were used to card the wool into cylindrical strips of downy, evenly distributed fiber. Holding a brush in each hand, the carder drew wool from one brush to the other, until the desired softness and evenness was achieved. If the brushing was insufficient, the result was knobby, uneven yarn, while over-brushing damaged the fiber.

Having learned how to card wool, the weaving apprentices moved on to spinning yarn. Yarn for carpets were spun in varying qualities—for carpet pile, warp threads, or yarn for weft thread. Pile yarn was usually spun from pure white wool intended for dyeing, and spun in varying degrees of tightness and thickness, depending on the desired density and fineness of the carpet. Black and gray wool were separated, then mixed with white wool for spinning warp and weft yarn or used in its undyed form for carpet pile. Like pile yarn, warp and weft yarns were produced in different qualities of tightness and thickness. Warp yarn threads were typically spun thin and tight, in contrast to weft yarn, which was generally spun thicker and looser. The thickness and tightness, or "twist" of each type of yarn determined the fineness of the finished carpet, the three yarns were spun accordingly.

After one to two years of carding wool and spinning yarn, apprentices would typically spend a full year or more learning to inspect and select raw wool before moving on to the carpet loom. Although selecting and preparing raw wool preceded carding and spinning of the yarn, apprentices had to acquire sufficient experience in carding and spinning before learning how to select raw material. The ability to differentiate the quality of raw wool at the shearing or purchasing stage was considered a crucial skill since wool quality ultimately determined the quality of the finished carpet. If inferior wool was used, neither wool spinning, yarn dyeing or fine weaving could turn it into a first-rate carpet. In short, a carpet was only as good as the wool used.

Assessing the quality of wool was not always easy, as there was considerable variation in wool sheared even from a single herd. In general, long, straight and thick fibers were preferred to short, crimpy wool, as was a high ratio of pure wool fiber to *drachu*, a coarse, hair-like fiber found mixed with wool that was brittle and not capable of absorbing dye well. The soft, lustrous wool from the sheep's under-

Saddling up for a journey.

neck was often sheared separately and fetched a higher price, whereas wool from the sheep's shoulders and upper legs, and wool matted due to excessive sheepskin grease, were considered least valuable. Each batch had to be inspected for impurities, and wool with large amounts of dirt or small stones fetched lower prices.

After the selection process, weaving apprentices helped to separate and wash the raw wool in preparation for carding and spinning. All-white wool, more abundant and valued for yarn dyeing, had to be separated from gray and black wool, which were either used undyed or dyed black with indigo. The preferred method of washing raw wool was in river water by hand, following which the wet wool was beaten with wooden sticks and dried in the sun.

INTERMEDIATE PHASE OF APPRENTICESHIP

An apprentice learned the rudiments of weaving by sharing a loom with an experienced weaver, and was often assigned to weave a narrow section of carpet under guidance. First he learned how to weave the drumtse knot, how to cut the loops of yarn knotted around the thin iron rod (*gyukshu*) to make a row of pile, and how to beat the row down using an iron tool resembling a claw (*chakshe*) and wooden hammer. He learned the order in which to weave the different colored yarn before learning how to tie each knot, and then how to execute simple designs independently by counting knots and rows while weaving. The apprentice learned how to produce a carpet from beginning to end, from preparing the mounting of the con-

A nomad in front of his yak-hair tent on the Changthang plateau.

tinuous warp and adjusting the loom, to crafting the tightly woven carpet fringe (*khapleb*) and cutting the finished rug off the loom.

During the apprenticeship, which lasted from two to three years, apprentices underwent practice, production, and instruction simultaneously; this allowed the master weaver to assess the apprentice's potential. Apprentices who showed no talent could be switched to full-time yarn spinning or trained in yarn dyeing, or they could return to their families. Apprentices with potential and ambition progressed to the next stage of independently weaving small rugs of simple geometric design, such as the traditional *shumi,* or "checkerboard." When they became proficient in weaving simple patterns, they moved on to more elaborate designs, such as the diamond-shaped amulet box pattern (*gawu*) and the more difficult medallion designs.

According to the late master weaver Wangdui, having learned the basic skills from assisting an experienced weaver, apprentices were expected on their own to study the art of proportion and color coordination necessary to render intricate designs such as dragons and phoenixes, snow lions, lotus flowers, and cloud patterns. Advanced techniques and "tricks of the trade" were closely guarded by experienced weavers, understandably, in their own professional interest.

At this level of skill, carpet designs were most commonly copied by looking at the backs of finished carpets, which were hung over the loom or rested on the weaver's lap for reference while weaving. Each knot and row of the sample carpet was meticulously studied, and refinements were made in proportion, choice of color, or knot counting, depending on the weaver's interpretation and taste. A weaver could improvise even as he worked, and most did. For example, a shade of yarn could run out before the carpet's completion, or the design had to be altered to accommodate the loom size. Just as often, weavers improvised for the sake of creative expression.

ADVANCED APPRENTICESHIP

During the advanced apprenticeship of weaving independently, a talented apprentice could not only "read" the backs of finished carpets and reproduce their design but was likely to introduce or reinterpret designs, thereby imparting a personal, coherent style and beauty to the new carpet. At this level of craft, design elements could be copied or adapted from Tibetan architecture, silk brocades, or the weaver could use his imagination to create new designs. If an apprentice demonstrated exceptional talent at this stage, the master weaver might assume an instructor's role, and choose to share secrets of the craft, including special techniques or the master weaver's personal style of interpreting and executing intricate designs.

Traditional Carpet Designs

The government guilds and commercial workshops often recruited mural artists and, in some cases, thangka painters who were trained in drawing actual-size carpet designs on traditional Tibetan handmade paper. These designs were drawn freehand, without markers or graph lines, and required considerable weaving skill to execute. The government guild workshop in Lhasa maintained several thangka painters to draw carpet designs and a complete set of their creations was kept stored at the guild workshop. Unfortunately, the whereabouts of this collection of original designs is not known.

Carpet weavers skilled in reading the special designs called *shokpo* interpreted and improvised as they wove, choosing yarn colors, calculating knots, and planning subsequent rows with the tying of each new knot. The Gabshi estate in the late 1940s could only claim two out of fourteen rug weavers who were skilled enough to weave from *shokpo*. It was at this advanced level of carpet weaving that individual expression became possible. Each woven carpet then became a creation of a distinct style and taste rather than a well-rendered reproduction. As with any creative vocation, true mastery was rare. Like the work of renowned thangka painters or master woodcarvers, carpets woven by true master weavers were highly valued and were in great demand by high lamas, government officials, and the aristocracy. Indeed, it was their patronage that contributed to the aesthetic refinement of the craft.

When an apprentice attained sufficient technical skill to read *shokpo* diagrams and execute intricate designs independently, he was graduated from apprenticeship and, upon application, formally recognized by the guild as a professional carpet weaver. As with the government guilds organized for woodcarvers, thangka painters, and other artisans, such professionals were responsible for carrying out orders placed by the government as service in lieu of tax, and in their spare time wove rugs for barter or sale at the local market. During the formal ceremony that marked admission into the guild, the weaver offered a silk scarf and *poma daisi* out of gratitude and respect to the guild director.

Sorting out the yarn.

The more Tibetan carpets one sees, the greater one's astonishment at the variety of their design, structure, and color combinations. A conviction begins to take root that these designers and weavers could keep producing original designs, creating new color arrangements, and improvising on structural proportion for eternity.

What explains the remarkable diversity of the Tibetan carpet? Most of all, it is the folk status of carpet weaving in Tibet. Until the mid-twentieth century, it should be remembered, Tibet was a conservative theocracy in which most of the art forms were religious in nature and thus subject to the formulaic specifications of Buddhist iconography. Unlike the exquisite sculpted images and religious paintings of Tibetan high art, carpets were mundane objects that were used pervasively by every social group. Though they had both ritual and functional uses in monasteries, they were too ordinary to figure in monastery murals or thangka depiction of Tibetan daily life. Ironically, it was the carpet's mundane status in a religious society that ensured its exemption from rigid prescriptions, which in the case of the Tibetan carpet would have produced something far less than what it became.

Consequently, the resulting artistic creativity unleashed is evident in any significant collection of Tibetan carpets. There are no two designs exactly alike, except for consecutively woven pairs and replicas specially commissioned. The uniqueness of Tibetan carpet weaving stems from this fact, and it explains why none of the major oriental weaving traditions produced anything comparable to the Tibetan carpet in terms of its diversity of design, color use, knotting structure, and above all the multitude of functions it served.

DIVERSITY OF TRADITIONAL USES
AND UBIQUITY OF THE BED-SIZE KHADEN

As remarkable as the diversity of Tibetan carpet designs are its diverse uses, from serving as seat covers for jeeps, bikes, and motorcycles, as well as neck-collars for dogs and yaks, or "crupper rugs" to protect donkeys' rumps from the chafing of harness straps. Tibetan carpets also serve as prostration mats, protective hangings, throne-covers, and back-rests, and they are just as commonly used as decorative wall hangings, door and window curtains, trunk and table covers, temple pillar hangings, riding blankets, and horse trappings.

Not only do these carpets serve every conceivable function but, in their most common form, the *khaden,* they have a daily use in virtually every Tibetan household. Ingeniously designed to adorn and to insulate, the khaden covers the low platforms that traditionally serve as beds by night and as brilliantly decorative

USE
AND
FUNCTION
OF
TIBETAN
CARPETS

Opposite: A room of the Dalai Lama in the Norbulingka.

couches by day. These bed-size carpets are just as commonly used in monks' quarters as in a peasant's adobe hut, a nomad's yak-hair tent, or an aristocrat's embellished living room. They are laid on the floor around low tables, their portability hinting at the "nomadic" origins of the craft.

Valued equally by peasant and noble, monk and nomad, the khaden rug represents a Tibetan's essential possession, a virtual birthright. In view of the immense popularity of rugs in Tibet and the multitude of their functions, the country can certainly be regarded as having a quintessential "carpet culture."

TIBETAN NOMADS AND WOOL

The cultural value of carpets in Tibetan society can be accounted for several factors, not the least of which is the Tibetan terrain and climate. The high plateau nurtured the evolution of wool's resilient fiber, protecting sheepskin from snow, wind, and temperatures below freezing. There is no doubt Tibetans have benefited enormously from their wool-craft, which enabled them to survive by making clothing, blankets, boots, grain bags, ropes, belts, animal trappings, and even a slingshot for the nomad boy tending livestock. Representing the technical and aesthetic pinnacle of centuries of indigenous wool-craft evolution, Tibetan carpet weaving is rooted in developments that ushered the replacement of animal skins by textiles for clothing and the use of woven tents for shelter.

By far Tibet's most valuable natural resource, wool, was for long its principal export. Indeed, it was partly to control this lucrative trade that the British invaded

A typical Tibetan living room with rugs, woven backrest pillows and hand painted frieze.

52

Tibet in 1904. Two distinct breeds of wool-producing sheep are found in Tibet: the aboriginal, pure-breed species that inhabit highlands at elevations above 14,000 feet and the mixed breed found in the river valleys of lower elevations. Tibetans traditionally make a distinction between the two varieties of wool produced: *changphel,* or "northern highland wool," and *yulphel,* or "valley wool." *Changphel,* produced far more abundantly, is long, coarse, and thick in diameter, whereas *yulphel* is short and fine, and preferred by Tibetans for garment textile weaving.

Sheared and supplied to the market by plateau-dwelling nomads, Tibet's highland sheep wool with its high lanolin content is exceptionally lustrous, and its length and thickness make it one of the world's best wool fibers for carpets. As a member of the vast continuum of nomadic wool-weavers stretching from Siberia to the Middle East, Tibetan nomads were undoubtedly the first to make practical use of this precious and plentiful resource. They were also probably first to weave carpets in the form of the tsukden planted pile on a portable back-strap loom. Since a constant preoccupation was to keep warm, tsukden was used as a source of insulation, spread on tent floors for sitting and sleeping on. To this day, they are woven and used by Tibetan nomads to keep warm and decorate their tents.

With the growing importance of sedentary agriculture, Tibetan wool-craft steadily flourished to become a principal occupation of farming villages. Though planting and harvesting seasons varied regionally, the long winter months were generally devoted to religious pilgrimage, local festivals, the making and drinking of *chang* (Tibetan barley beer), and wool-craft. Carpet weaving became widespread in central and southern Tibet, notably in the Nyang River valley region of Tsang province, where, in the 1930s and1940s, every household in every village owned at least one loom.

Endowed with Tibet's most fertile soil, Tsang's relative prosperity permitted use of the best materials and equipment, and also the leisure time for high quality weaving. Eventually, village carpet weaving spread almost throughout Tibet, whereas nomadic weaving remained confined to the tsukden carpet and textiles for tents, bags, blankets, and garments. As carpet weaving spread and it became more refined, demand burgeoned for carpets of all sizes and shapes by temples and monasteries, wealthy nobles, and for the private chambers of the Dalai Lama.

Ecclesiastic Use of Tibetan Carpets

Carpets of different sizes were woven for monasteries for uses that were esoteric, ritual, and mundane. These monastery rugs could generally be distinguished by their ecclesiastical colors: saffron or red, and golden yellow or orange. As in most parts of Tibet, the bed-size khaden for sitting and sleeping were the most common rugs. Of the same width as the bed-size rug but longer, the runners called *tsokden* were spread out in assembly halls and chapels, with rows of cushions on which monks sat when they recited prayers, performed rituals, and received teachings. Monks brought their own rugs from home to sleep on in their monastic cells, the quality and design of the rugs reflecting the monk's family background. Lamas and senior monk officials, though, were more likely to have specially woven carpets provided by the monastery or offered as gifts by lay supplicants.

A *tsokden* temple runner was traditionally a long carpet with individual segments of repeating motifs, such as lotuses and medallions, each segment marking the space for a sitting cushion. The repeating patterns could be incorporated in a single arrangement or divided into discrete segments to resemble a long row of square sitting rugs.

Two distinct types of carpets were woven to adorn the seats of high lamas: *khagangma,* a square or rectangular sitting mat about half the size of a khaden, and a scallop-shaped carpet designed to cover throne back-rest of the lama. These rugs typically sported Buddhist symbols reflecting the lama's stature, such as the *yungdrung* (swastika), the ritual implement *dorje.* or dragons, phoenixes, or snow lions holding flaming jewels. Such ceremonial rugs were used only during special religious rites or teachings that the lama was expected to attend.

According to the late Mingmar Wangdui, a former master weaver at Gyantse, designs for monastic carpets were often specified. Lamas who had artistic training might occasionally draw sketches or write out instructions for carpet designers. Although monastic estates often employed village weavers to work in lieu of paying grain tax, it was more common throughout Tibet to contract out to the estate workshop of an aristocrat. In the 1940s, Wangdui recalled, such a special order— a throne back-rest for the Dalai Lama—was woven by the leading master weaver of Gyantse Dunji, Tibet's first government weaving guild. When the carpet was presented, there was an uproar: it was thought the central design of a pair of dragons facing each other, with a phoenix in between, could be interpreted to symbolize polyandry, which, of course, would be highly inappropriate for use by the Dalai Lama.

Other carpets produced for monasteries include the decorative *kathum,* or "pillar rugs," used as adornments on pillars and usually depicting a dragon chasing a flaming jewel. Wall hangings, as well as covers for drums and tables, were primarily decorative too. According to the late master weaver Wangdui, wall hangings and sitting rugs depicting human skulls, skeletons, and flayed skins were occasionally

A one-loom workshop in
a private home.

ordered for the meditation chapels of monasteries. They were often used in esoteric Buddhist rituals, generally by itinerant monks and tantric practitioners.

Tiger pelt rugs, known as *bokchak,* were sometimes used for similar esoteric or ritual functions. The flayed tiger skin signified the subjugation of the otherwise untameable ego by the meditative path of Buddhism. According to Tibetan oral tradition, tiger pelt rugs were primarily used as *bonjo,* which was draped over the possessions of high lamas and government officials on long journeys on the backs of mules, yaks, and horses. They were also used as talismans placed above temple entrances, most notably at the Norbulingka, the Dalai Lama's summer residence. Woven in pairs, these small carpets covered cylindrical cushions and were hung on both sides of temple entrances.

CARPETS AND ARISTOCRACY

The Tibetan nobility too used the carpet in ways that were decorative, ceremonial, and ritual. Carpets for everyday use included a khaden for each bed, sometimes two or three stacked together. Special khaden were used during New Year celebrations, weddings, and other auspicious occasions. Square khagangma were unrolled to honor special guests and placed on top of khaden in reception rooms. Other carpets found in aristocratic homes included door curtains (*goyo*) in place of textile door hangings, covers for back-rest pillows (*gyabnye*) and arm cushions, decorative table covers, wall hangings, and window curtains resembling *goyo* in design and shape. Like the bed-size khaden, curtain carpets for doors and windows provided warmth and were pleasing to look at.

THE YABSHI PHUNKHANG CAVALRY RUGS

The eleventh Dalai Lama Khedup Gyatso was born in 1838 in Kham to the Phunkhang family, which became Tibet's Yabshi, or first family, and later a part of the highest circle of Lhasa nobility. The Monlam Torgya held in Lhasa annually on the twenty first day of the first lunar month following the New Year was the most grand and all-important festival, the purpose of which was to drive away evil spirits and to usher in the New Year. The highlight of the festival was a stunning parade of cavalry to which only the most noble of the aristocracy were invited and only a number of participants from each family based on status. The cavalry were adorned in ancient armor, helmets with peacock plumes, and armed with lances and swords. Their horses were decorated with pomp, including a set of saddle rugs to match the occasion.

As a daughter-in-law, Phunkhang Diki Dolma of the Yabshi Phunkhang family tells it, the paraphernalia for each detachment of the ceremonial cavalry was stored and maintained by a designated family, which included a set of exquisite saddle carpets that would be used only once a year. Yabshi Phunkhang was a cabinet minister in 1930s, and as a matter of prestige, he had a set of Mongolian-style saddle rugs made for the Phunkhang detachment of twenty-four horses. These saddle rugs were woven at the family's Gyantse estate, where Phunkhang's eldest son, the county head, had established a small carpet-weaving workshop. The rugs produced were identical, woven in the traditional oval Mongolian shape with a central medallion to symbolize longevity. They also carried the Tibetan inscription *Yab-Phun-Ta-Mak,* or "the Cavalry of Yabshi Phunkhang."

Many decades later, a saddle carpet with the clear inscription of Yabshi Phunkhang cavalry fell into the hands of a collector. This was a rare find as the provenance of very few Tibetan carpets can be conclusively proven. It seemed this and a few other pieces had been sold by the Tsunmo Khangsar family of Lhasa, which eventually reached collectors in Nepal and the United States. Even more fascinating, these carpets were entwined to a significant historical event in Tibet's modern history known as the Reting Conspiracy.

In 1937, four years after the thirteenth Dalai Lama passed away, and the fourteenth Dalai Lama had not come of age to take over, the senior lama official Reting Rinpoche was appointed Regent, and became the single most powerful

A monk seated on a temple runner.

authority in Tibet. In 1941, following this power struggle, Reting Rinpoche was ousted from his position and placed under house arrest. Yabshi Phunkhang, like others associated with the Regent's faction, came under suspicion and was stripped of his official position by the new Regent, Taktrak, though he was eventually cleared of wrong-doing and rehabilitated.

How the Tsunmo Khangsar family in Lhasa came to have in its possession a few of these saddle carpets from Yabshi Phunkang's estate is that during the period of Yabshi Phunkhang's fall from grace, one of his younger sons was married into the

A nomad on the
Changthang plateau.

Tsumo Khangsar family. Presumably he took a few of the phung cavalry rugs with him as his contribution to the marriage.

TIBETAN FLOOR CARPETS

Only the nobility and high lamas commissioned oversize floor carpets called *sapden*. They were used at special ceremonies and receptions, but they were rarely woven due to the limited width of the traditional Tibetan loom. Also, Tibetans did not customarily use large carpets as floor coverings. On rare occasions commissioned for nobles and high lamas, Tibetan sapden were produced under the direction of experienced master weavers at production centers of aristocratic estates or government workshops.

Since most rooms in Tibetan houses require central posts to serve as ceiling supports, large floor-coverings acquired from Turkestan or China were often cut into khaden-size pieces or were made to accommodate ceiling posts by snipping out one or more holes in the center of the carpet. For the same reason, Tibetan sapden were woven in separate, customized pieces until the 1940s and 1950s, when estate and government workshops began building wide looms for specially commissioned sapden. The traditional method of weaving sapden in separate pieces persisted as late as the 1950s, however. A large floor rug was ordered for the newly renovated Norbulingka Palace from the Lhasa guild workshop around this time. The guild's looms were too narrow, and so the wide floor carpet was woven in four separate pieces and sewn together.

CARPETS FOR EQUESTRIANS

If khaden is the most ubiquitous of Tibetan carpets, what follows it in extent of use is the *taden,* or "saddle carpet." Like the khaden, the saddle carpet provided warmth and comfort, and it was also used as an adornment by every class of Tibetans, from simple farmers to the Dalai Lama himself. Mules, horses, and yaks were the principal means of transport in Tibet until 1950. Then one working vehicle appeared, but even the capital, Lhasa, had no paved roads. Like Mongolians and other nomadic peoples of Central Asia, Tibetans have since antiquity been equestrians, who in all probability had used some form of the saddle carpet ever since learning the art of pile weaving.

These carpets for horses, mules, and yaks acquired many curious forms. They were decorative as well as ingeniously practical trappings found nowhere else, such as the bell collar, forehead decoration, and harness crupper rug. Saddle rugs were woven in sets of two, a smaller one was used above the saddle whereas the larger was used to cushion the horse below the saddle. Another larger, often more elaborate horse blanket was used to cover the horse at rest in the stable. Tibetan saddle carpets take three dominant forms: the oldest are oval shape resembling Mongolian saddles; a distinctly Tibetan rectangular shape; and a butterfly shape, in recent times the most popular of the three, copying the shape of British saddle cloths at the turn of the century. Khaden-size luggage covers for transport animals, signifying rank and prestige, were also used by high lamas and officials for long journeys.

VILLAGE CARPET WEAVING

Village weaving, mostly limited to khaden, khagangma, and taden, represents the survival of the craft in its most traditional form, a simple function of economics. The quality of yarn spinning, dyeing, and weaving on aristocratic estates was generally superior to that of villagers' homes because the nobility could afford to recruit the best craftsmen and provide the best equipment and material. In the countryside, common folk wove primarily for their own needs and occasionally sold or bartered what they made. Thus, the carpets generally reflected the economic well being and the tastes of the weaving household or locality.

Generally, villages unable to afford the best wool, dyes, and equipment, produced relatively modest carpets, with simple, geometric designs and very few colors. Unable to afford the large wooden looms required to weave the Tibetan knotted-pile drumtse, other villages used simple back-strap or horizontal frame-looms to weave the more primitive tsukden as well as garment textiles. And yet, it was village carpet weaving that contributed significantly to the remarkable spectrum of carpets, in variation of material and design, befitting the truly local means and tastes of weaving families, villages, and regions. Many a humble farming household produced drumtse carpets of such distinction to make an aristocrat envious. It is the spirit and creativity of weaving carried out so pervasively in the humble household of Tsang region, farmers and semi-nomads alike that made rug weaving into a form of Tibetan national folk art. The subsequent increase in demand by the wealthy monasteries, merchants, and commoners throughout Tibet gradually changed this craft into an increasingly important handicraft industry.

TIBETAN RUG WEAVING IN THE MODERN ERA

The economic landscape of twentieth-century Tibetan rug weaving is radically different from that of the past. By the mid-1980s in post-Cultural Revolution Tibet, international trade had become a possibility. The potential of the international market abroad was vastly more extensive than that offered by Tibet's limited population. However, entering the fiercely competitive international market requires modern management and organizational skills coupled with market-sensitive aesthetic judgment and exacting quality control, all of which were in short supply in Tibet. Those were the reasons that propelled co-author Kesang G. Tashi to take on the challenge of producing Tibetan carpets in their homeland.

The rug-weaving tradition in Tibet has now been revitalized from the devastating period of the Cultural Revolution. Today, Tibet has many more carpet factories, each with more weavers than the early workshops that belonged to the weaver's guild or any of the old Phala and Doring estates. However, as a commercial enterprise, the carpet industry in Tibet is still minuscule compared to that of Nepal.

In view of the fact that Nepal did not have rug-weaving tradition until the Tibetans started the carpet industry there in the 1960s, the progress made within Tibet is not laudable. A major obstacle in Tibet is a problem of perception. As a handicraft industry, rug production has yet to be treated seriously. It is not considered modern or progressive and therefore employment in it lacks prestige. Furthermore, in Tibet as elsewhere in the developing world, the carpet industry as an investment option, is too often overshadowed by the many, infinitely more seductive, get-rich-quick investment schemes, whether real or illusory. Until the carpet industry is recognized, within Tibet, for its social benefits of generating employment, providing training, and instilling cultural pride at the most basic levels of Tibetan society, further growth is likely to be slow. Perhaps, however, a gradual and sustainable growth may prove to be better in the long run.

The long-term strategic goal of a the carpet industry in Tibet must be to maintain the highest quality of product. As a landlocked economy, Tibet cannot compete successfully on price point and volume with its limited rug production. Therefore, the uniqueness of Tibet's rug-weaving heritage must be upheld at all cost. Traditional hand-carding and hand-spinning of northern highland sheep wool, the choice of designs and colors, and a host of other characteristics discussed in these pages all contribute toward making a Tibetan rug an authentic Tibetan cultural artifact. Simply put, the newly woven rugs produced in their Tibetan homeland must aspire to be the collectable antiques of tomorrow. They must be as well made and as true as the antique rugs that are appreciated for their unique Tibetan character. Preserving this distinctive rug-weaving heritage is an important element of preserving the very essence of Tibet's cultural identity.

ༀ། །རྒྱལ་ཚེ་ཨ་རྒྱལ་པོ་རྫས་ར
རྗེ་གནས་ཆེ་ལོག་ཀྱུ་ཁྱི་བག་
འཚོ་པ། ༡༣༥

Antique painting showing
traditional Tibetan rug
patterns.

This collection of slings woven with wool and yak hair in archaic designs represent the earliest Tibetan wool-craft, dating back to the founding of Tibetan civilization, which began with the domestication of sheep and yak.

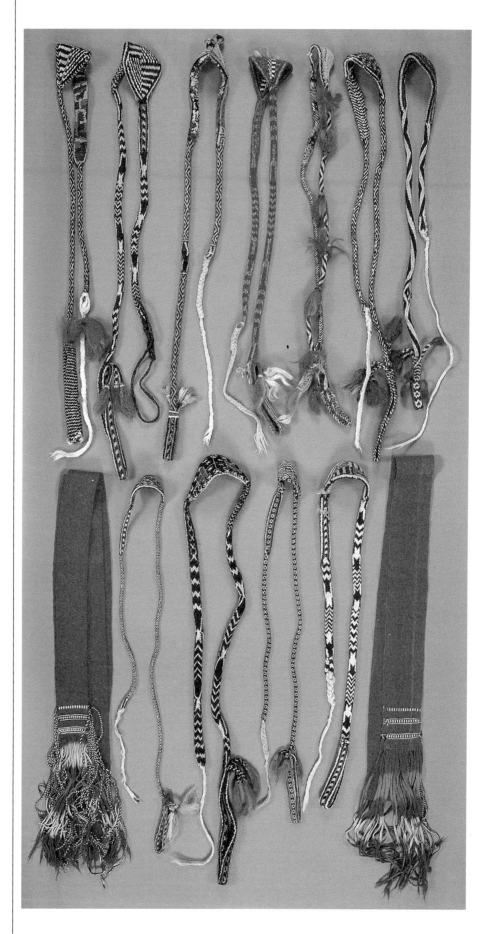

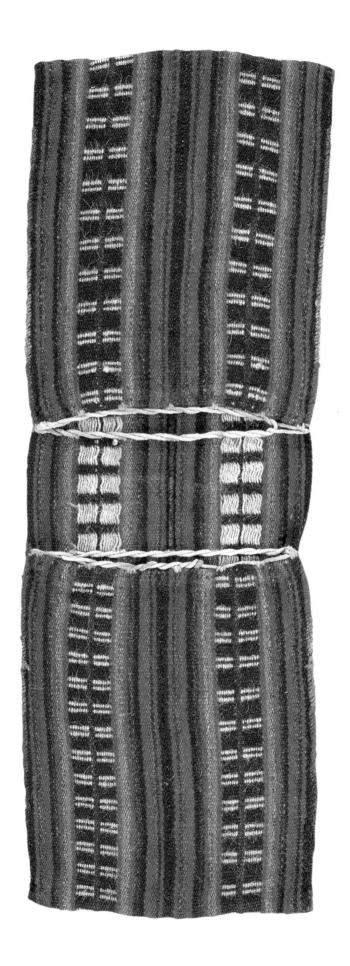

This nomad's bag is woven using the same technique as Tibetan tents, using a back-strap loom that produces narrow strips of flat-weave material.

Nambu is the most popular Tibetan textile, used to make clothing, aprons, and blankets. Its dense weave provides warmth against the cold and bitter wind.

An example of a nambu chuba, a Tibetan robe.

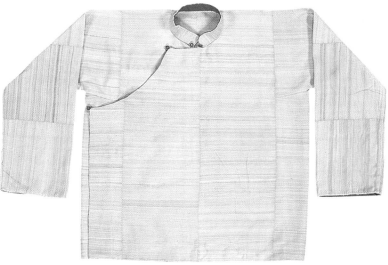

This jacket is made of sherma, the finest of Tibetan textiles. A full day of concentrated weaving is needed to produce twenty by eight centimeters of cloth from the hand-spun yarn, athough the dense fabric will last for generations. Unfortunately, the sherma weaving tradition is not likely to last.

Tsukdruk is the earliest form of Tibetan textile utilizing the planted-pile technique, and is thus the predecessor of the Tibetan pile rug as we know it today. Tsukdruk is woven in narrow strips on back-strap looms, and most commonly used for blankets and winter clothes.

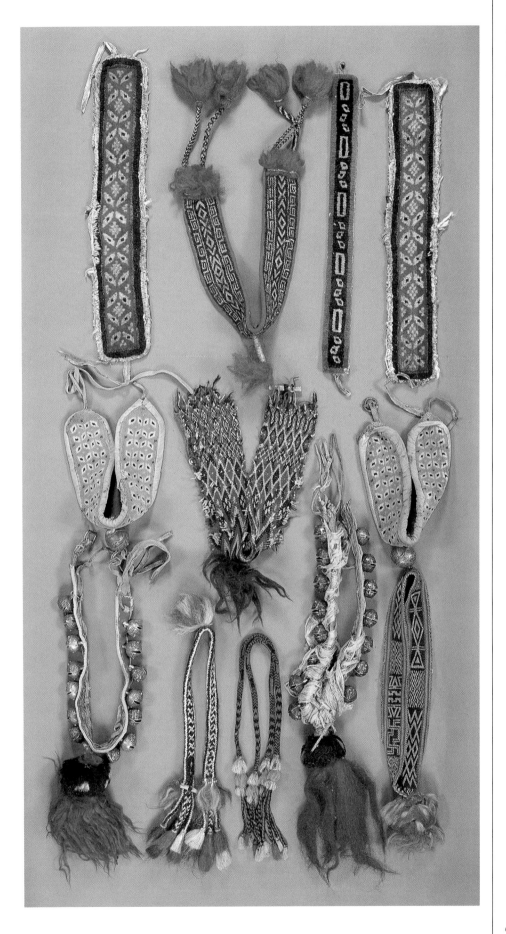

A collection of decorative animal trappings woven in both flat weaves and pile weaves.

Horse ornaments called takyab are used as decorative and auspicious trappings to cover the forehead of horses and mules. The woven motifs include wish-fulfilling gems and other symbols of good fortune.

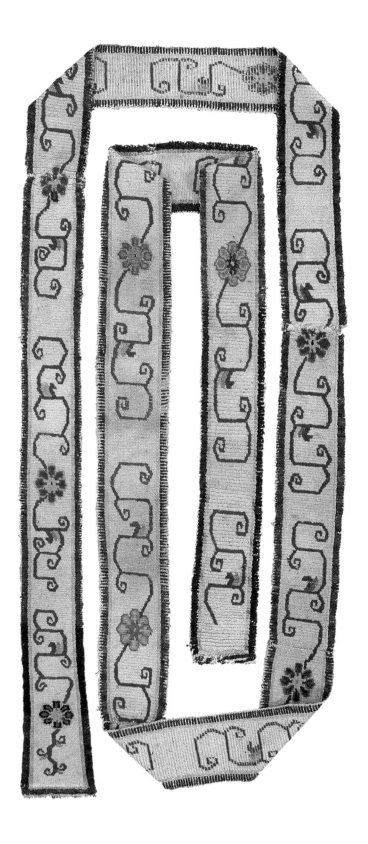

The only rug of its kind ever seen by the author was used in the Tsang village to decorate the wall like a frieze. Such wall treatments in Tibet are usually painted, and may have occasional textile decoration. Using a rug in this manner was a custom of the distant past and limited to the weaving towns in Tsang. This rug, woven with archaic stylized lotuses and swirling branches, is made up of five separate pieces sewn together. The looseness of the weave, archaic design, and its unusual function rarely found today make this the oldest rug illustrated in this book. Wall frieze rug, Eighteenth to nineteenth century, natural dyes, wool weft, wool warp, 6 cm x 775 cm.

An excellent example of a Wangden drumtse of loose weave and archaic design, a rug type dating back to the tenth century. Layered borders frame the central field, two primitive mandala-like designs flanking a gawu, a design derived from a Tibetan amulet box. Wangden drumtse like this continue to be woven today in the far-flung regions of Tibet. Nineteenth century, natural dyes, all wool, 83 cm x 152 cm.

Another example of the warm and folksy Wangden rug still woven in distant villages of Tsang. The triple mandala-like medallions, the use of a simple but bold meander border, and the loose weave are typical of archaic Wangden style. Early twentieth century, natural dyes, all wool, 70 cm x 140 cm.

A classic Wangden khagama square with archaic mandala-like medallion framed by a meander border. Nineteenth to twentieth century, natural dyes, all wool, 64 cm x 68 cm.

An archaic geometric pattern of simple window-like panels framed by four bands of border, including a wide meander border. The rich warm colors of red, blue, white, and green, plus the thick wool pile make this an treasured rug in the Tibetan winter. Nineteenth century, natural dyes, all wool, 62 cm x 64 cm.

A classic Wangden rug with a yungdrung in the center framed by border bands of red and black, then yellow and black, following the prescriptions of Lama Jamyang of Wangden village where this rug type is believed to have originated. Nineteenth to twentieth century, natural dyes, all wool, 75 cm x 75 cm.

This Wangden rug with central double-dorje design follows the strict prescriptions for ecclesiastic use as laid down by Lama Jamyang. The dorje, a ritual implement used by monks, symbolizes the indestructibility of wisdom. Though loosely woven in only three colors, there is beauty in the economy of this rug. Wangden khagama. Nineteenth to twentieth century, natural dye, all wool, 70 cm x 77 cm.

This Wangden rug effectively uses linked yung-drung and additional bands of color to frame the central motif of a double dorje, a remarkable achievement accomplished through extremely loose weaving. Wangden khagama. Nineteenth to twentieth century, natural dye, all wool, 77 cm x 84 cm.

A rare and excellent
example of an early
Kamdrum, a type of rug
that originated in Kampa
Dzong and preceded the
full-fledged Tibetan
drumtse. The three
archaic mandala-like
medallions are a com-
mon motif in early
Tibetan rug design. Here,
linking yungdrung frame
the central field in a dramatic oval, to which
additional meander
designs at the four cor-
ners of the central
medallion add emphasis.
Kamdrum Khaden, nine-
teenth to twentieth cen-
tury, natural dyes, wool
weft, wool warp, 86 cm x
158 cm.

The back side of the
Kamdrum opposite,
showing the detail of
its weave.

A delicate checkerboard rug, using extremely small squares. The simple, narrow red border frames the rug perfectly. One of the oldest rugs illustrated in this book. Khaden, early nineteenth century, natural dyes, wool weft, wool warp, 81 cm x 194 cm.

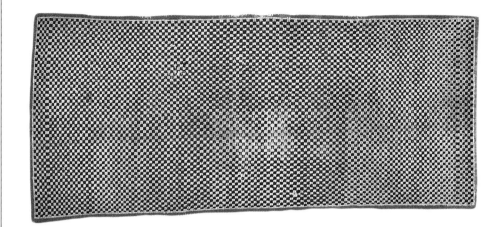

A similar geometric design of repeated gawu in black. The pink color used has faded. Early twentieth century, natural dyes, wool weft, cotton warp, 92 cm x 157 cm.

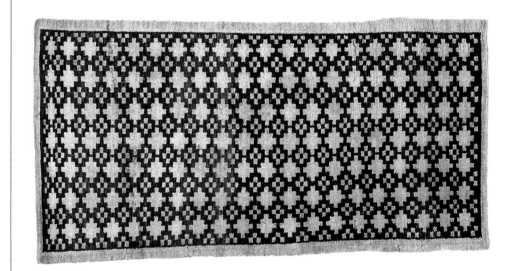

The archaic Tibetan design called gawu, derived from a protective amulet box, is delicately repeated in tan and black. Khaden, early twentieth century, natural dyes, wool weft, wool warp, 94 cm. x 160 cm.

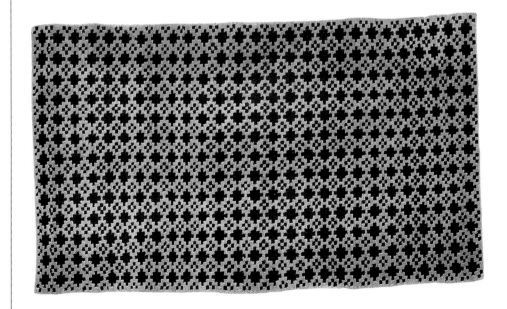

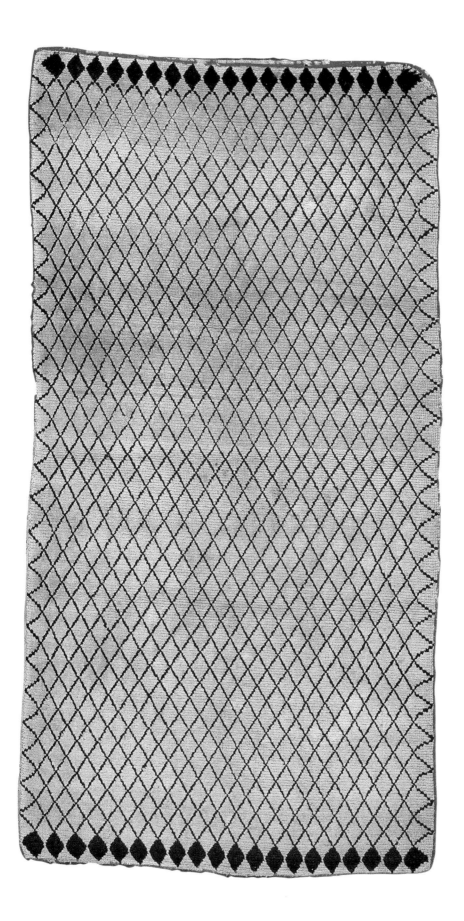

A rare and exquisitely subtle rug, perfectly executed. The skillful use of natural dark brown and white wool is superb. The design of the lattice chain is strikingly similar to the ancient iron lattice curtain chain in front of the Maitreya Buddha in Jhokhang, Lhasa. This rug may have been commissioned by a lama to use either as a door curtain or a ritual partition to demarcate a sacred space. Nineteenth century, natural wool color, wool weft, wool warp, 86 cm x 167 cm.

A delightful checkerboard rug with mellow shades of red and blue evenly worn. Checkerboards are typically associated with picnics and other festive occasions. Late nineteenth century, natural dyes, wool weft, wool warp, 93 cm x 178 cm.

A pair of eye-catching-blue and white checkerboard rugs. The simplicity of these rugs makes them adaptable to most decorative environments. Early twentieth century, natural dyes, wool weft, cotton warp, 89 cm x 167 cm.

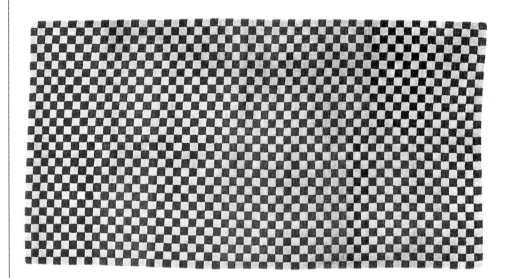

A mate to the blue and white checkerboard rug above. Early twentieth century, natural dyes, wool weft, cotton warp, 89 cm x 167 cm.

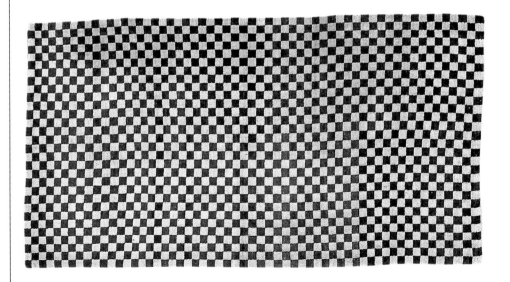

This exquisite rainbow checkerboard rug has the striking visual appeal of modern Western op-art. Many Westerners are surprised by the contemporary appeal of some traditional Tibetan designs. Khaden, nineteenth to twentieth century, natural dyes, wool weft, cotton warp, 89 cm x 147 cm.

Some of the weaving villages in Tsang choose to leave a wool fringe around their rugs, perhaps due to nostalgia for Wangden styles. Delicate bouquets of stylized flowers in the central field are framed by multiple borders, with design, colors, and weave all skillfully executed. Early twentieth century, natural dyes, wool weft, wool warp, 77 cm x 162 cm.

The five separate squares of this checkerboard rug were never separated. Most likely, it was used as rug for picnic outings where barley beer and sho, a dice game provoking much merriment, were enjoyed. Early twentieth century, natural dyes, wool weft, cotton warp, five units of 34 cm x 40 cm.

This small checkerboard rug was used to cushion a horse below the backstrap just above the crupper. The rug typically served as a functional and a decorative piece. Horse trapping, cushion, early twentieth century, natural dyes, wool weft, cotton warp, 38 cm x 38 cm.

This exquisitely designed and skillfully woven geometric is definitely the work of a master weaver with the highest standards. Khaden, nineteenth to twentieth century, natural dyes, wool weft, wool warp, 70 cm x 153 cm.

This fringed, wool pile rug features triple medallions enclosed in a complex border of frames and floral elements. The delicate design and overall quality of the weave make it an outstanding example of the weaver's craft. Nineteenth to twentieth century, natural dyes, wool weft, wool warp, 79 cm x 159 cm.

Three lotus medallions rest on a beige field surrounded by floating yungdrungs and eternal knots, all symbols sacred to Buddhism, enclosed by a meander border. Khaden, early nineteenth to twentieth century, natural dyes, wool weft, wool warp, 76 cm x 166 cm.

This popular design features a repeated, stylized four-petal floral element within framed lozenges, and hints of Turkish influence via the Silk Roads. The outermost simple guard stripe is associated with Tibetan rugs of an earlier period. Khaden, late nineteenth century, wool weft, wool warp, natural dyes, 88 cm x 180 cm.

Another example of the popular, repeated four-petal floral motif within framed lozenges. The meander pattern of the outer border blending into linked Buddhist yungdrung and the orange field indicate ecclesiastic ownership. Khaden, nineteenth to twentieth century, natural dyes, wool weft, cotton warp, 83 cm x 164 cm.

This rug makes skillful use of layered tones of indigo blues, while its flared shape and elegantly elongated design of branching lotuses and lotus leaves indicate it was likely used as a door curtain. Early twentieth century, natural dyes, wool weft, cotton warp, 160 cm, by 81 cm (top width), 87 cm (bottom width).

A simple design of red peonies on a field of green. The rich, ruby red achieved with brilliant use of madder and the textured forest-green field with traces of yellow is achieved by adding rhubarb yellow over indigo. The small corduroy patch is a telling indicator of a lack of rug repair technique. Nineteenth to twentieth century, natural dyes, wool weft, wool warp, 89 cm wide.

This delicate design of peonies on an ivory field has a hand-sewn border of imported felt from British India, which was added at a later date. Khaden, early twentieth century, natural dyes, wool weft, cotton warp, 78 cm x 151 cm.

The main decorative
elements of this rug are
lotuses and double-
dorje-like floral motifs,
both so stylized as to
blend together seam-
lessly. The four corners
appear as stylized
incense smoke swirls
ornamented with lotuses,
while the outermost
border as well is formed
with an assortment of
floral and auspicious
emblems. Early twentieth
century, natural and
aniline dyes, wool weft,
cotton warp, 75 cm x
56 cm.

This elegant rug of unusual size features in its center a mythical animal and may have been inspired by a Chinese textile used to ornament a table. Table cover, early twentieth century, natural dyes, wool weft, cotton warp, 58 cm x 137 cm.

This densely woven rug is
enhanced by an elaborate
design of full, half, and
quarter medallions.
Within the medallions
are Buddhist yungdrung
motifs and auspicious
symbols with the sylized
Chinese character for
longevity at the center.
Well-placed clusters of
three auspicious fruits
in the blue field and a
rich red border complete
the elegant and formal
design. Khaden, early
twentieth century, natural
dyes, wool weft, cotton
warp, 66 cm x 150 cm.

This dramatic rug in deep indigo blue was likely woven on a noble estate of Gyantse, and includes design elements from three neighboring cultures. The multi-medallion concept is from Chinese textiles; the yungdrungs and mandala-like motifs within the medallions are Tibetan; and the stylized floral petals are probably of Turkish influence via Khotan. Khaden, early twentieth century, wool weft, wool warp, natural dyes, 85 cm x 160 cm.

This rug of multi-medallion design superimposed on a field of intricate linking yungdrung was most likely woven on an estate of Tsang nobility. Khaden, early twentieth century, natural dyes, wool weft, wool warp, 75 cm x 142 cm.

This perfectly woven rug depicts an idealized scene from nature, a flock of black-necked cranes, today an endangered species in Tibet. Khaden, early twentieth century, natural dyes, wool weft, wool warp, 88 cm x 165 cm.

Two pairs of dragons and phoenixes are depicted on a deep blue field, each dragon pursuing a flaming gem. In the center is a grand indigo-blue lotus with beautiful green branches stretching toward the phoenixes. The hand-sewn protective maroon corduroy is a reminder that this otherwise majestic rug has a utilitarian function. Early twentieth century, natural dyes, wool weft, cotton warp. 91 cm x 149 cm.

A well-composed triple dragon rug with archaic Tibetan gawu medallions framed by borders of increasing complexity. The green dragons are complemented by an outer green border with eight scholarly emblems. Nineteenth to twentieth century, natural dyes, wool weft, cotton warp, 79 cm x 129 cm.

A center panel features three dragon medallions with floating cloud motifs and stylized incense smoke swirling in the four corners. The rainbow colors of an inner border are framed by an outer border of bold linking yungdrung in a meander pattern. Nineteenth to twentieth century, natural dyes, wool weft, cotton warp, 78 cm x 165 cm.

Since Tibetans often make and use rugs in pairs, antiques in original pairs are much sought after. This Chinese brocade-inspired design is attributed to the late minister Kapshopa, and is thus called Kapsho pesar (Kapsho's new design). Early twentieth century, natural dyes, wool weft, cotton warp, 93 cm x 70 cm.

Mate to the Kapsho pesar rug above, a style very popular in Lhasa of the 1920s, which was enjoying a renaissance of Tibetan rug weaving. It became fashionable for the nobility in Lhasa not only to produce rugs, but also show off the new designs created by their weavers. Early twentieth century, natural dyes, wool weft, cotton warp, 93 cm x 70 cm.

This pair of rugs featuring triple crane medallions is beautifully composed. The choice of scholarly emblems with swirling ribbons gives the rug an elegant flowing movement, while an elaborate border combining panels of birds and geometric motifs gives it a charming finish. Early twentieth century, natural dyes, wool weft, cotton warp, 86 cm x 165 cm.

Mate to the rug with triple crane medallions above. Early twentieth century, natural dyes, wool weft, cotton warp, 86 cm x 165 cm.

A pair of whimsical rugs with a central mandala-like medallion surrounded by a profusion of branching auspicious fruits and lotuses. The weaver could not resist adding two pairs of dragonflies to the delightful botanical surroundings. Early twentieth century, natural and aniline dyes, wool weft, cotton warp, 88 cm x 164 cm.

Mate to the rug above with a central mandala-like medallion surrounded by auspicious fruits and lotuses and two pairs of dragonflies. Early twentieth century, natural and aniline dyes, wool weft, cotton warp, 88 cm x 164 cm.

Pair of gyabney, or cush-
ion-cover rugs, used as a
backrest on a bed with
matching khaden. The
vases symbolize fulfill-
ment and are positioned
above motifs of sacred
Mount Meru rising above
the universe of the three
elements: oceans, moun-
tains, and clouds. Early
twentieth century, natural
and aniline dyes, wool
weft, cotton warp, 42 cm
x 67 cm.

Mate to gyabney above.
Early twentieth century,
natural and aniline dyes,
wool weft, cotton warp,
42 cm x 67 cm.

A central crane medallion is surrounded by four butterflies and a rather plump phoenix in each corner. Early twentieth century, natural dyes, wool weft, cotton warp, 80 cm x 148 cm.

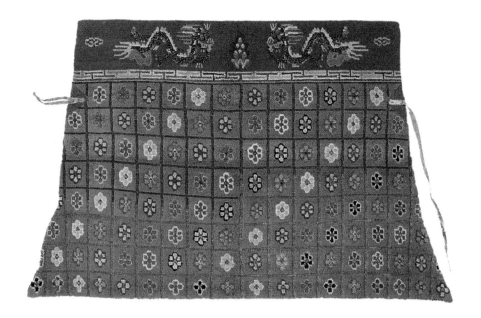

A handsome horse blanket for the ecclesiastic nobility with repeat stylized lotus petals within indigo frames. The upper band is composed of two dragons flanking a wish-fulfilling gem on a rich maroon field. The border features the same shades of green, gold, maroon, blue, pink, and white as the lotus petals of the field. The leather strapping is intact and in position for use. Horse blanket, early twentieth century, natural dyes, wool weft, cotton warp, 103 cm x 138 cm x 88 cm.

This horse blanket of dominant maroon was woven in a Tsang village for a local customer. The branching lotus with colorful leaves is balanced by elements of sky, earth, ocean, and fire in the lower two corners. The upper band of the meander border is followed by a wider border with more branching flowers. Horse blanket, early twentieth century, wool weft, cotton warp, natural dyes, 94 cm x 128 cm x 71 cm.

This rug of repeated window-panel motifs with meander and outer red borders is what remains of a larger horse blanket. The owner must have salvaged a larger damaged rug to make a sitting rug. Shugden, early twentieth century, natural dyes, wool weft, cotton warp, 58 cm x 82 cm.

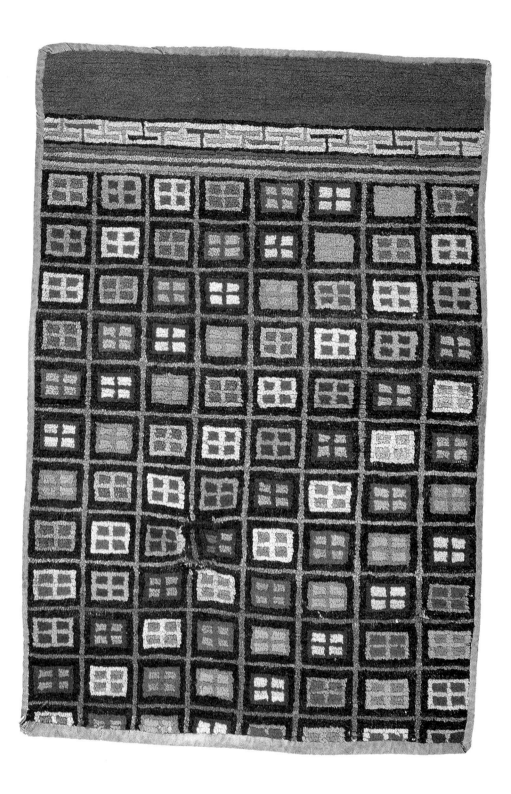

This unusual rug features a design called pema chakdro, meaning lotus in iron lockets. The lotus design is a popular Buddhist motif, symbolizing human potential, as it grows out of mud to attain perfection. Early twentieth century, wool weft, cotton warp, natural dyes, 73 cm x 131 cm.

In this rug with popular lotus and vine design, the green field stands out, while the thin but pronounced symmetry of the vines is perfectly woven and the meander border frame elegantly finishes the piece. Khaden, early twentieth century, natural dyes, wool weft, wool warp, 77 cm x 160 cm.

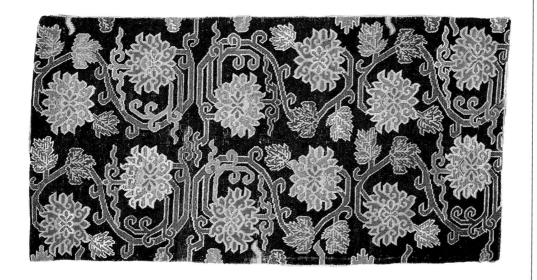

A classic design called pema chuni, or twelve lotuses, became popular again in the 1930s, when rug weaving enjoyed a renaissance. At that time every aristocratic estate had its own weavers and produced its own signature designs. Early twentieth century, natural dyes, wool weft, cotton warp, 90 cm x 179 cm.

As evidence of the popularity of the pema chuni design, a variation with a beige field is included here. Khaden, early twentieth century, natural dyes, wool weft, cotton warp, 81 cm. x 173 cm.

Here the popular and worldly pema chuni design is presented on an appropriately ecclesiastic field of orange, so that even an ascetic monk can enjoy it. Khaden, early twentieth century, natural dyes, wool weft, cotton warp, 85 cm x 162 cm.

Another striking triple medallion rug with three archaic gawu occupying the center field, its four corners ornamented with stylized lotuses and leaves, the whole surrounded by multipe frames and stylized floral and frog-foot motifs. The outermost border is filled with floral and scholarly emblems. Khaden, early twentieth century, natural dyes, wool weft, wool warp, 73 cm x 140 cm.

This predominantly orange and maroon double medallion rug with several complex and ornamental borders has a distinctive Khotanese flavor, while the segmentation into two khagama-like frames gives it the look of a monastic runner. Khaden, early twentieth century, natural dyes, wool weft, cotton warp, 82 cm x 140 cm.

This monastic pillar rug features a five-clawed imperial dragon on an orange field holding a flaming gem above the Tibetan universe of clouds, mountains, and waves. In the center is the sacred Mount Meru. Above the dragon is an intricate canopy. A hand-sewn silk border has been added. Pillar rug, early twentieth century, natural dyes, wool weft, cotton warp, 137 cm x 70 cm (top), 82 cm (bottom).

Although not identical, this rug and the example opposite may be from a larger set of similarly designed pillar rugs made for the same monastery assembly hall. While the position and execution of clouds is more awkward in this example, the alternating green panels on the canopy and additional shades of red and blue added to the Mount Meru motif are definite improvements. Pillar rug, early twentieth century, natural dyes, wool weft, cotton warp, 129 cm x 69 cm (top), 81 cm (bottom).

Two imperial dragons in flight with a flaming gem against an orange sky above the clouds of sacred Mount Meru. The stylized cloud-band border with dramatically rendered ocean waves frames this rug perfectly. Khaden, early twentieth century, natural dyes, wool weft, cotton warp, 92 cm x 172 cm.

This majestic presentation of a phoenix in flight in a rust sky of floating clouds is said to have come from the Norbulingka, originally the Summer Palace of the Dalai Lama. Although such a claim cannot be easily proven, the rug was most definitely used by an ecclesiastic person of the highest rank. Khaden, early twentieth century, natural dyes, wool weft, cotton warp, 88 cm x 181 cm.

This ecclesiastical rug boasts an opulent rust-colored field filled with stylized cloud motifs. The particulalrly rich texture of the rust field is caused either by two separate dye lots or by an uneven twist in the yam. Khaden, late nineteenth century, natural dyes, wool weft, wool warp, 87 cm x 188 cm.

This predominantly orange door-curtain rug belonged to an ecclesiastical personage. The three vases of textured indigo blue sprouting bouquets of auspicious fruits and lotuses form the central motif, while additional ornamentation includes the lotus, conch, eternal knot, and a tiger (top), which has been partially cut off. Border motifs are stylized clouds, mountains, and waves. Early twentieth century, natural dyes, wool weft, cotton warp, length 204 cm, top width 92 cm, bottom width 99 cm.

A fitting rug for a learned geshe, a Tibetan scholar-priest, featuring triple medallions in an rust-colored field surrounded by floating scholarly emblems, stylized lotuses, and auspicious fruits. Khaden, early twentieth century, natural dyes, wool weft, cotton warp, 88 cm x 162 cm.

This unusual rug of what appears to be multiple skull patterns was claimed by its previous owner to have been a personal possession of the Regent Reting. Whatever the merit of this claim, the uncommon design was likely a commissioned rug by an ecclesiastic personage. Khaden, early twentieth century, aniline dyes, wool weft, wool warp, 65 cm x 190 cm.

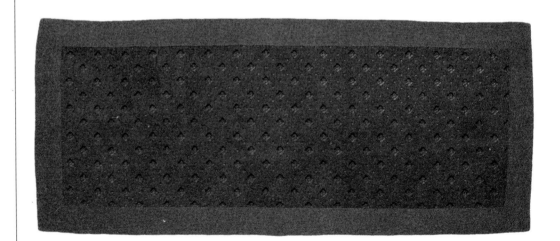

This abstract tiger rug is one of several pictured here said to have come from the estate of the Reting Rinpoche, who was Regent during the fourteenth Dalai Lama's minority and is known to have surrounded himself with beautiful objects. This tiger rug is exceptional in color and design, and could only have been made by a master weaver and an equally sophisticated commissioner. Khaden, early twentieth century, natural dyes, 88 cm x 70 cm.

Orange throne backrest of an ecclesiastic noble. A pair of beautifully designed phoenixes dominate the stylized cloud, mountain, and wave motif, including a towering Mount Meru surrounded on three sides by some of the eight auspicious symbols. Throne backrest, early twentieth century, natural dyes, wool weft, cotton warp, 64 cm x 76 cm.

Rust-colored throne backrest rug with a pair of grand snow lions offering wish-fulfilling gems. Above a mythical animal holds a garland of lotus flowers glorifying the dharma. The border below is the stylized cloud, mountain and wave motif with Mount Meru; a border of the eight auspicious symbols surrounds the three sides. This design is appropriate only for a high ecclesiastic person. Throne backrest, early twentieth century, natural dyes, cotton weft, cotton warp, 82 cm x 84 cm.

A rare oversize Tibetan rug, sapden, in ecclesiastic rust and maroon. This is the maximum size of floor covering practical for traditional pillared Tibetan architecture. Four imperial dragons and two smaller phoenixes surround two guardian snow lions, while a border of linked yungdrungs dramatically frames the maroon sky with floating clouds. This rug is said to have belonged to the estate of the Regent Reting. Sapden, early twentieth century, natural dyes, wool weft, cotton warp, 182 cm x 215 cm.

The only Tibetan silk rug ever seen by the author, believed to have been commissioned for a new Norbulingka palace completed in 1953. The bottom of the rug depicts the stylized clouds, mountain, and wave motif with Mount Meru. The center highlights two phoenixes making an offering of a lotus bouquet and are symbols of longevity appropriate for the highest-ranking lama of the land. Mid twentieth century, aniline dyes, cotton weft, wool warp and silk pile, 65 cm x 124 cm.

A set of saddle rugs. This smaller top rug depicts a pair of snow lions engrossed in play with a flaming gem, while the larger bottom rug (opposite) accommodates two pairs of snow lions. Saddle set, top piece, early twentieth century, natural dyes, wool weft, cotton warp, 60 cm x 74 cm.

In both pieces of the saddle-rug set, the frame is rendered in half-floral bands of alternating colors, while the outer borders are deep blue fields with majestic dragons and phoenixes. Saddle set, bottom piece, early twentieth century, natural dyes, wool weft, cotton warp. 63 cm x 126 cm.

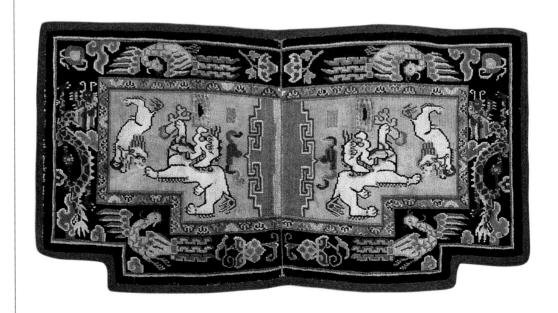

This saddle rug set is a good example of those used by common villagers. Here the subject and the colors are more earthy and robust, and lack the sophistication of the nobility or wealthy merchants. Saddle set, top piece, twentieth century, natural dyes, wool weft, cotton warp, 57 cm x 74 cm.

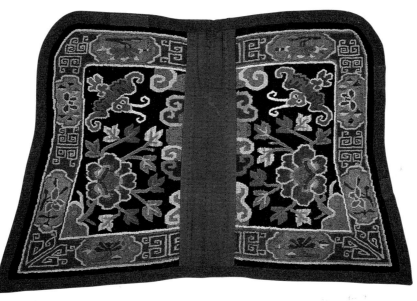

The lower piece of a saddle rug set typically reflects and presents in duplicate the motifs of the upper piece. Here, two bats are added to the profusion of flowering branches, reflecting the influence of Chinese motifs, in which the bat symbolizes luck. Saddle set, lower piece, twentieth century, natural dyes, wool weft, cotton warp, 59 cm x 97 cm.

123

Three saddle rugs from a set of twenty woven in the 1920s for the cavalry of Yabshi Phunkhang, which was invited by the Tibetan government to participate in the annual New Year parade, an honor accorded only to the highest-ranking nobility. Tibetan rugs such as these, incorporating written evidence of their age and provenance, are rare. Saddle rugs, wool weft, cotton warp, 62 cm x 119 cm, 64 cm x 123 cm, 62 cm x 115 cm.

Saddle rug showing rich glowing colors and a skillfully woven design of archaic dragon medallions surrounded by floral bouquets, lucky bats, and symbols of eternity. The border features eight scholarly emblems. Saddle rug, early twentieth century, natural and aniline dyes, wool weft, cotton warp, 58 cm x 50 cm waist x 134 cm.

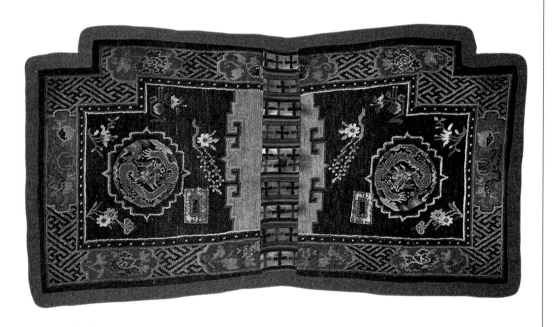

Classic dragon medallions are surrounded by auspicious fruits and lotuses studded on an intricate linking yungdrung border. The two panels are joined by a nambu textile filler. Such exquisitely designed and woven saddle rugs highlight the equestrian culture of Tibet. Saddle rug, early twentieth century, natural dyes, wool weft, cotton warp, 66 cm x 150 cm.

This rug with a pair of
majestic dragons and
gems has been well used
and well cared for, as
evidence by the rein-
forcement of a rather
distracting blue cotton
border. Saddle rug, early
twentieth century, natural
dyes, all wool, 120 cm x
98 cm x 76 cm.

A bottom saddle rug
with dragon medallions
and branching lotuses
surrounded by an ele-
gant, gem-lined inner
border and an outer bor-
der of eight additional
dragons. Saddle rug. Early
twenty century, natural
dyes, wool weft, wool
warp, 122 cm x 96 cm x
75 cm.

A saddle rug with double Khotanese medallions and an ornate linking yungdrung border studded with intermittent lotus flowers. The medallions are surrounded by stylized botanical motifs in the central field and the four corners. Saddle rug, early twentieth century, natural dyes, wool weft, cotton warp, 130 cm x 62 cm x 68 cm.

A saddle rug with two Khotanese-influenced medallions surrounded by highly stylized botanical motifs. The three frame borders consist of pearl drops, a meander, and delicate scholarly emblems, auspicious fruits, and cloud motifs. A silk strip has been sewn on to protects the edges. Saddle rug, early twentieth century, natural dyes, wool weft, cotton warp, 67 cm x 155 cm.

127

This striking saddle rug has the name of its owner woven in, but the script is not legible. Saddle rug, early twentieth century, natural dyes, wool weft, cotton warp, 68 cm x 152 cm.

Saddle rug with stylized botanical renderings. Early twentieth century, natural dyes, wool weft, cotton warp, 66 cm x 152 cm.

A saddle rug in maroon and rust. The central field has two gawu medallions surrounded by sparkling white belak motifs, with stylized branching lotuses in the four corners. The framing is pearl drop, meander, then linking yungdrung studded with intermittent lotus flowers. Saddle rug, early twentieth century, natural dyes, wool weft, cotton warp, 108 cm x 122 cm x 69 cm.

The fourth Khotanese medallion saddle rug shown has the distinct feature of different color schemes in its two halves. The green is achieved through an indigo dyeing followed by a soaking in rhubarb yellow. However, for the second half, the dyer may have used up his indigo supply, and the result is the yellow only. Saddle rug, early twentieth century, natural dyes, wool weft, cotton warp, 68 cm x 156 cm.

A pair of small rugs sewn together to be used as a saddle rug for a smaller animal, possibly a donkey. This design of stylized flower petals within a field of repeat lozenges is called pema chakdok, or lotus in iron lockets. Early twentieth century, natural dyes, wool weft, wool warp, 42 cm x 42 cm, 42 cm x 42 cm.

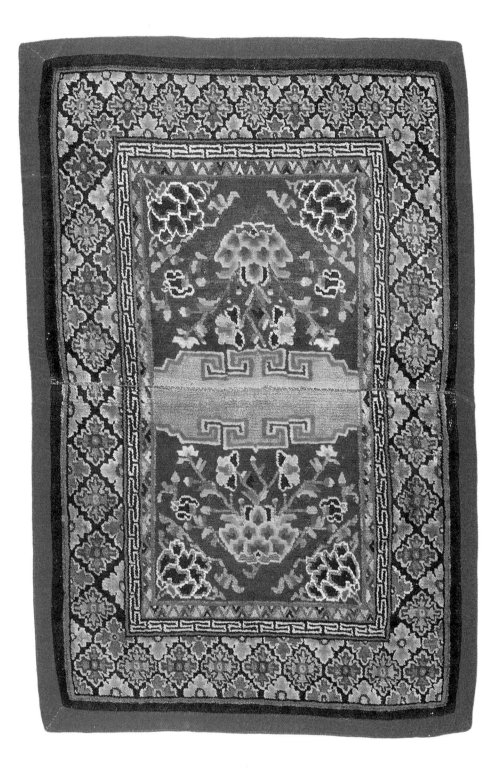

This top saddle rug in rich jewel tones with multiple frames features an elaborate Khotanese border enclosing a central field of delicate floral bouquets. Saddle rug, early twentieth century, wool weft, cotton warp, 61 cm x 93 cm.

A five-clawed imperial
dragon with flaming gem
accompanied by an
equally regal phoenix
with a branching lotus in
its beak appear to be
performing a ritual dance
among the clouds, a
motif suitable for a high
lama. Khagama, early
twentieth century, natural
dyes, wool weft, cotton
warp, 80 cm x 88 cm.

Stylized floral pattern
rug. Shugden, early twen-
tieth century, natural
dyes, wool weft, wool
warp, 55 cm x 76 cm.

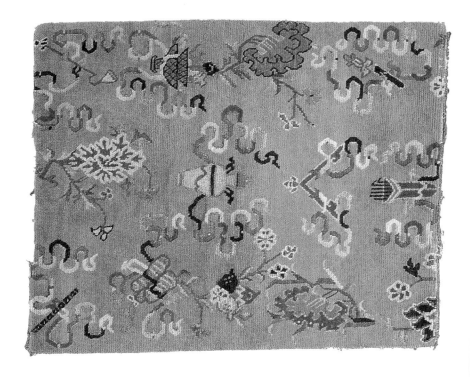

A perfectly woven pictorial rendition of eight scholarly emblems ornamented with auspicious fruits and lotuses, a fitting rug to honor a geshe, a scholar-priest. Shugden, early twentieth century, natural dyes, wool weft, cotton warp, 60 cm x 74 cm.

An elegant sitting rug with multiple medallions in a rust-colored field. The core of the medallion is a simplified mandala, a Buddhist celestial architectural form often elaborately depicted in thankas. Shugden, early twentieth century, natural dyes, wool weft, cotton warp, 58 cm x 82 cm.

133

A very attractive shugden woven masterfully with excellent design and color composition. Eight lotuses of blue, red and green are perfectly positioned against the background of intricately swirling branches and leaves. Owned by an ecclesiastic noble. Shugden, early twentieth century, natural dyes, wool weft, cotton warp, 59 cm x 77 cm.

A classic gawu central medallion circled by belak or frog foot motifs. The corners are embellished with Turkish-inspired stylized floral and branches. Five frames of elegant borders with the final one being filled with stylized floral and scholarly emblems. Khagama, early twentieth century, natural dyes, wool weft, cotton warp, 65 cm x 75 cm.

134

A central gawu medallion is surrounded by stylized floral motifs in four corners framed by meander borders. Shugden, early twentieth century, natural dyes, wool weft, cotton warp, 54 cm x 66 cm.

Multiple Khotanese geometric motifs are surrounded by a bold meander border. Shugden, early twentieth century, aniline dyes, wool weft, cotton warp, 60 cm x 72 cm.

A central medallion of mandala-like design is surrounded at the four corners by stylized incense smoke swirls. The pearl drop border in blue is framed outside by an elegant border of alternating half-geometric gawu. Khagama, early twentieth century, natural dyes, wool weft, wool warp, 65 cm x 67 cm.

A magnificent dragon with a striking mane holding four flaming gems. The surrounding clouds and two borders give this rug a dramatic presence. Shugden, early twentieth century, natural dyes, wool weft, cotton warp, 60 cm x 74 cm.

A rare rendering of a dragon smaller than its companion phoenix, both cavorting around a lotus medallion with swirling branches and colorful leaves on a rug quite worn from use. Shugden, early twentieth century, natural dyes, wool weft, cotton warp, 60 cm x 81 cm.

A pair of regal dragons, each holding two flaming gems, soaring through the sky above stylized clouds, mountains, and ocean wave motifs with Mount Meru looming in the distance. Shugden, early twentieth century, natural dyes, wool weft, cotton warp, 58 cm x 73 cm.

A dynamic pair of dragons engaged in their ritual competition for the flaming gem in deep blue sky with rich cloud formations. Shugden, early twentieth century, wool weft, cotton warp, natural dyes, 59 cm x 77 cm.

Rug for a back rest with a pair of dragons making a wish-fulfilling gem offering on a green field ornamented with flaming gems and stylized clouds. Gyabney, early twentieth century, natural dyes, wool weft, cotton warp, 36 cm x 63 cm.

A charming sitting rug in green, with a majestic dragon and phoenix in ritual play. A large branching lotus usurps the space of the smallish phoenix. Shugden, early twentieth century, natural dyes, wool weft, cotton warp, 61 cm x 88 cm.

Snow lion playing with a gem with a vase of flower ornaments behind him. In the distant background is the Tibetan landscape framed by a meander border. Gyabney, early twentieth century, natural dyes, wool weft, cotton warp, 40 cm x 63 cm.

This alternating bird and lotus medallion is finely knotted to achieve its delicate design, while the less than perfect use of indigo adds charm. Shugden, nineteenth or early twentieth century, natural dyes, wool weft, wool warp, 56 cm x 80 cm.

A central medallion depicting a dharma-chakra, the Buddhist symbol of the eight-fold path, is framed on two sides by dramatic wave and mountain motifs with Mount Meru looming, and on two sides with elaborate Khotan border designs. Shugden, early twentieth century, natural dyes, wool weft, cotton warp, 58 cm x 80 cm.

This rug was inspired by
a Chinese tapestry, and
features a central symbol
of longevity, auspicious
bats and the eight schol-
arly emblems. The dis-
tortion in the weaving
adds charm to the
design. Early twentieth
century, natural dyes,
wool weft, cotton warp,
56 cm x 69 cm.

An intriguing rug with a very worn but regal presence a chessboard in red and yellow, evidently well used through the ages, perhaps by men with military power, framed by a dramatic linking yung-drung border. Khagama, early nineteenth century, natural dyes, cotton weft, cotton warp, 78 cm x 85 cm.

This unusual rug design with an extraordinary luster was likely brought in from the Ningxia region as a gift for a Lhasa noble. It is thus called in Tibet gyarum, meaning Chinese rug or simply foreign rug. Khaden, early twentieth century, aniline dyes, cotton weft, cotton warp, 78 cm x 151 cm.

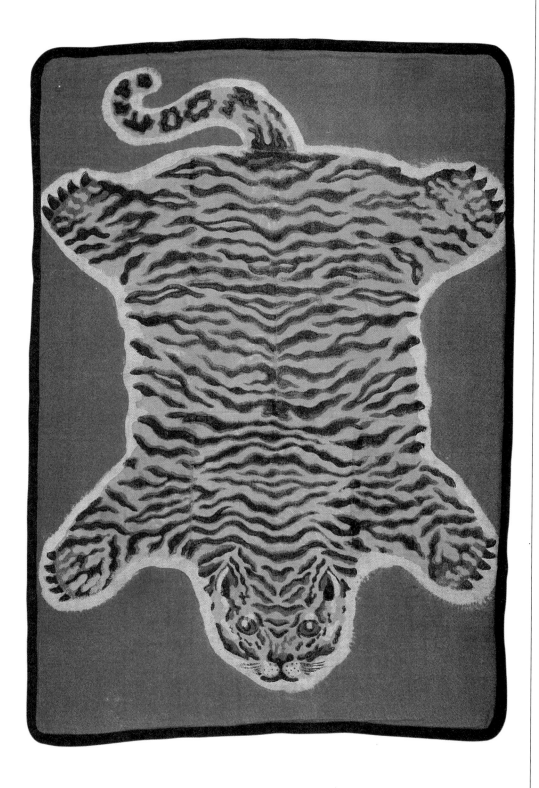

This unusual textile piece with tiger design is believed to have been a gift from Mongolia, with which Tibetans have always enjoyed close cultural ties. Early twentieth century, all wool, 120 cm x 164 cm.

A rare and unusual flat-weave textile made to be used like a pile rug but incorporating a central piece of valuable imported Bhutanese textile obviously treasured by the family. Khaden, early twentieth century, all wool flat weave, 88 cm x 120 cm.

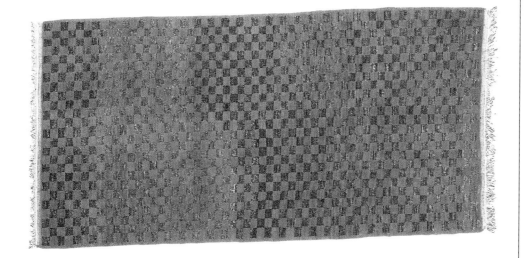

Blue and red checkerboard from the Gangchen Folk Arts Collection. Khaden, 1998, natural dyes, wool weft, wool warp, 61 cm x 91 cm.

Blue and cream linking yungdrung, from the Gangchen Folk Arts Collection. Khaden, 1998, natural dyes, wool weft, wool warp, 63 cm x 92 cm.

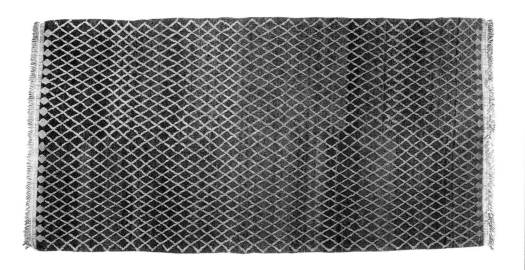

Blue and cream lattice chain from the Gangchen Folk Arts Collection. Khaden, 1998, natural dyes, wool weft, wool warp, 61 cm x 94 cm.

Lotus medallion on a field of green surrounded by lotus and vines from the Gangchen Folk Arts Collection. Khaden, 1997, natural dyes, wool weft, wool warp, 63 cm x 92 cm.

150

Top: Khawachen, Lhasa where Gangchen carpets are woven.

Bottom: *Liwus* and *tsukdruks* in the courtyard.

Glossary

bokcha Tiger runner used to protecting an entrance.

bonjo Rug or textile used to cover and protect.

bodhistsattva Sanskrit term for an enlightened being who has vowed to help all sentient beings attain enlightenment.

chakshe Hand carding tools spiked with wire.

chang Tibetan beer made of fermented barley.

changphel Northern Highland wool from sheep grazing above 14,000 feet.

chap lug or **chap shub** An ornamental textile bag to hold a ritual vase, worn by Tibetan priest.

chuba Tibetan native costume for men and women.

den A Tibetan word for mat for the floor; generic term for carpet

dorje Vajra in Sanskrit, a ritual implement or symbol of it that symbolizes great wisdom.

drumtse A securely knotted Tibetan pile rug.

dzipa A flat-weave woven with yak hair commonly used to make Tibetan nomadic tent.

gabney Stuffed cushion used as a back rest, and the pile rug that typically decorates it.

gamdrum Knotted pile rug that originated in Gampa Dzong in Tsang.

gawu An amulet box containing sacred objects, worn for protection, or the stylized pattern based on its shape.

gelukpa "Virtuous ones," or the reformed school of Tibetan Buddhism, often called the "Yellow Hats."

geshe Highest formal degree earned by a scholar-monk in the Tibetan monastic university.

goyo Door curtains, whether textiles or pile rugs.

gyuk shu A unit of knotting.

kamdrum Early pile rug that originated in the town of Khampa Dzong.

kathum Rug used to decorate monastery pillars.

khaden A standard size Tibetan carpet of approximately three feet by six feet.

khagangma A square rug of approximate three feet.

khapleb Two hand-sewn sides of a rug.

la drim Refers to knotted-pile carpet which some speculate had its origin in Ladakh.

la drum Refers to drumtse or pile carpets believe to come from Ladakh.

liwu A coarse flat weave.

losar Traditional Tibetan New Year.

mandala An architectural design depicting the Buddhist view of the cosmos.

namdruk Another Tibetan word for nambu, or woolen textile.

nambu Traditional Tibetan woolen textile woven on narrow looms, popularly used to make coats and gowns.

norbu Precious gem.

pangden Portable textile loom that rests on the weaver's lap; also, a woven textile used to make women's aprons.

pema Lotus.

pesar New design or new style.

phel-lek Wool-craft; including all wool-related crafts such as carding spinning, and weaving.

ra kulu Goat cashmere.

ra pu Goat hair.

samadrok Semi nomadic people in Tibet.

ring pu Literally "long," referring to long wool fringes on primitive Tibetan rugs.

sang A unit of Tibetan currency.

sapden A carpet or a mat for the floor.

sherma A finely woven wool serge fabric used for making clothing.

shokpo Technical drawing of a rug design.

shugden A small sitting rug used for honored guests.

taden Saddle rug.

takgyab Ornamental pile rug used to decorate the foreheads of mules and horses.

thangka Tibetan Buddhist paintings in the form of portable scrolls.

thukpa A Tibetan word for a generic noodle soup.

treche Literally "knife cut," in reference to a primitive cut-loop pile rug.

tsampa Roasted barley flour, a staple of the Tibetan diet.

tsokden Long runner-like rugs used in the monastery assembly halls.

tsukden A primitive form of piled rug that proceeded a full fledge securely knotted pile rug.

tsukdruk A piled textile commonly used as blankets and bed covers.

Wangden drumtse Primitive form of drumtse or pile rug that originated in Wangden.

Yabshi First family, referring to a family that has given birth to a Dalai Lama.

yak kulu Yak cashmere.

yulphel Softer wool from sheep grazing below 13,000 feet.

yungdrung Swastika motif used in Tibetan Buddhism.

Bibliography and Sources

ENGLISH SOURCES

Bidder, H., *Carpets from Eastern Turkistan,* [Teppiche aus ost Turkestan], Tubingen, 1964

Denwood, Philip, *The Tibetan Carpet,* Aris and Phillips Ltd, England, 1974

Goldstein, Melvyn, *A History of Modern Tibet,* University of California, Berkeley, 1989

Hou, S. Z., *Tibetan Archaeology,* Tibetan People's Publishing House, Lhasa, 1990

Kuloy, H.K., *Tibetan Rugs,* White Orchid Press, Bangkok, 1982

Laufer, B., *Loan words in Tibetan,* Sino-Iranica, Field Museum of Natural History Publication 201, Chicago, 1919

Shakabpa, W.D., *Tibet, A Political History,* Yale University Press, New Haven, 1964

Stein, R.A., *Tibetan Civilization,* Stanford University Press, Palo Alto, California 1972

Yang, S.W., An Xu and Sonam Gyentsen, *Tibet's Drumtse,* Handicraft Administration Bureau Publication, Lhasa, 1984

TIBETAN SOURCES

Pawo Tsukla Tringwa (Dpa'-bo Gtsug-lag-phreng-ba), *Mkhas pa'i dga' ston* ["The feast of the learned one"], Tibet, sixteenth-century text

Taranatha Jetsun (Tara-na-tha Rje-Gtsun), *Nyang Chos 'byung* ["The spread of dharma in Nyang Valley"], Tibet, sixteenth-century text

Tsang Nyong Heruka (Gtsang-smyon He-ru-ka), 'rNal 'byor gyi dbang phyug dam pa rje btsun mi la ras pa'i rnam par thar pa dang thams cad mkhyen pa'i lam ston ["Biography of the venerable yogi Mi-la ras-pa"], Tibet, fifteenth-century text

INTERVIEWS WERE CONDUCTED WITH

Master weaver Gyen Mingmar Wangdui, Lhasa, 1990
Master weaver Gyen Troloy, Lhasa, 1992
Master weaver Gyen Yunten, Gyantse, 1991
Kusho Taring Jigme, Lhasa, 1992
Kusho Phunkhang Diki Doma, Lhasa, 1992

About the Authors

Trinley Chodrak began his classical Tibetan education at the age of eight. From 1954 to 1958 he studied at the National Institute of Minority Studies, Beijing, where he continued to pursue his interest in Tibetan studies. The years 1959 to 1992 were dedicated to editorial work at Tibet Autonomous Region's Peoples' Publications, Lhasa, where he later became chief editor. He was appointed the Director of Tibet Autonomous Region's Tibetan Museum in 1993. Chodrak is national recognized scholar of Tibetan culture; he has published numerous books on the subject, including *Geography and Sites of Tibet* and *My Native Home, Tibet,* and has translated eight major volumes on Tibetan studies.

Kesang G. Tashi is a Tibet-born graduate of Dartmouth with a master's degree from the University of Wisconsin, Madison. In 1986, Tashi left a career in international banking in New York with the goal of developing a sustainable commercial enterprise that would make a positive impact in Tibet. He was instrumental in revitalizing Tibet's rug-weaving heritage by developing the Gangchen carpet of Tibet, which has gained recognition in the international market. In 1995 he returned to his native Gyalthang and built the Gyalthang Dzong Hotel where the emphasis is on promoting ecotourism and Tibetan culture. Tashi is currently working to expand the hotel into a mountain resort with eco-lodges and health-spa facilities. He is an avid trekker and squash player, and resides in Riverdale, New York, with his wife and two children.

INDEX

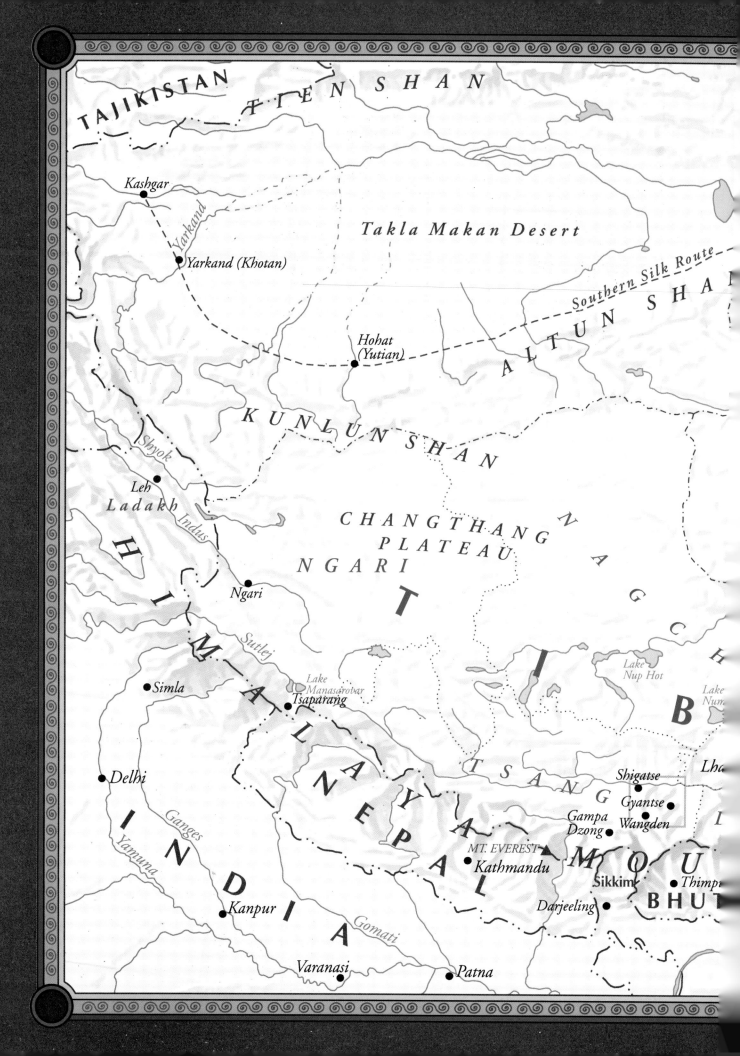